GUN
CONTROL

GUN CONTROL

Threat to Liberty
or Defense Against Anarchy?

Wilbur Edel

PRAEGER

Westport, Connecticut
London

Library of Congress Cataloging-in-Publication Data

Edel, Wilbur.
   Gun control : threat to liberty or defense against anarchy? /
Wilbur Edel.
     p. cm.
   Includes bibliographical references and index.
   ISBN 0–275–95145–6 (alk. paper)
   1. Firearms—Law and legislation—United States. 2. Gun control—
United States. I. Title.
KF3941.E25 1995
344.73'0533—dc20   94–25311

British Library Cataloguing in Publication Data is available.

Library of Congress Catalog Card Number: 94–25311
ISBN: 0–275–95145–6

First published in 1995

Praeger Publishers, 88 Post Road West, Westport, CT 06881
An imprint of Greenwood Publishing Group, Inc.

Printed in the United States of America

The paper used in this book complies with the
Permanent Paper Standard issued by the National
Information Standards Organization (Z39.48–1984).

10 9 8 7 6 5 4 3

Copyright Acknowledgments

The author and publisher gratefully acknowledge permission to reproduce the following
material:

Excerpts from *The Gallup Poll: Public Opinion 1980*, Scholarly Resources edition, 1981
volume, p. 31.

Szulc, Tad. Excerpts from "Dispatches from Eastern Europe, Warsaw, Poland, May 4."
National Geographic (March 1991): 15.

Excerpts reprinted from the September, 1989 issue of *Field and Stream* by permission of
Field and Stream Magazine, pp. 15–16.

Reagan, Ronald. Excerpts from "Why I'm for the Brady Bill." *New York Times* (29 March
1991). Copyright © 1991 by The New York Times Company. Reprinted by permission.

To the unforgettable
Mrs. Ed

Contents

Acknowledgments

I am indebted, as always, to Bucknell University Library and to Tom Mattern and other members of the library's technical staff for their unfailing assistance in identifying and locating source materials. Many thanks are due Nancy Pack Palmer for her critical reading of the entire manuscript and for the valuable suggestions she contributed to both the substance and style of the work. A final bow goes to Gloria Mincemoyer, whose computer and typing skills made possible the preparation of a presentable manuscript and who gave unusual care and patience to the tiresome task of proofreading.

For permission to quote from articles on the subject of gun control, I am grateful for the courtesies extended by *Field and Stream* magazine, The Gallup Organization, the *New York Times*, and Tad Szulc and the *National Geographic* magazine.

Introduction

In the United States much of the literature on gun control has been written to prove that laws governing the manufacture, sale and/or possession of firearms are either unconstitutional or constitutional, ineffective or essential to public safety, un-American or vital to the protection of a democratic society. Each side has its enthusiasts and its prophets of doom. Those who insist on strict control see the alternative as breeding a society in which the law of the jungle will prevail. Advocates of free trade in weapons warn that government interference will undermine the constitutional guarantees of personal freedom and, ultimately, lead to dictatorship.

The battle over controls is a constant one at all levels—national, state and local—and is fired by conflicting attitudes that are influenced by tradition, fear and widely divergent concepts of personal liberty and the limits of government responsibility. Thus, the people of Morton Grove, Illinois, approve a ban on all private possession of handguns, and the city council of Kennesaw, Georgia, counters with an ordinance that *requires* the head of every household to own a gun and to keep a supply of ammunition on hand.

The most serious challenge to government regulation of firearms developed in 1994 when a movement to organize private militias spread to more than half of the states. Spurred by passage of the Brady bill, the 1994 crime bill, and the disastrous firefight between federal agents and members of the Branch Davidian sect in Waco,

Texas, leaders of the movement see these events as part of a conspiracy to deprive citizens of their constitutional right to keep and bear arms and, ultimately, to destroy the entire Bill of Rights by extending government controls to every aspect of life. To protect themselves and the nation against such tyranny, militia leaders are training recruits in the use of arms and are stockpiling assault weapons and ammunition in anticipation of a final showdown. Their purpose is expressed openly, and their activities are widely advertised, as documented in an October 1994 report by the Anti-Defamation League entitled "Armed and Dangerous: Militias Take Aim At The Federal Government," and by the film clips shown on "CBS This Morning," November 21, 1994.

To do justice to this problem I have felt it necessary to go back to the origins of American notions of personal liberty and the purpose of government. That is why the story begins with a review of the traditions that settlers of the first thirteen colonies brought with them from the mother country, which, for the majority of colonists, was England.

Subsequent chapters trace the development of constitutional and municipal laws relating to the private possession of guns and the striking change in public attitudes and social conditions that has occurred, in this country and abroad, over the past fifty years. The vigorous—often rancorous—debate sparked by this change poses a serious challenge to the American people. Suggestions for meeting this challenge are offered in the concluding chapter.

1

Our European Heritage

It all started centuries ago in England, long considered the mother country of the thirteen colonies nestled on the eastern shore of North America. But in the England of precolonial days, the right to bear arms, while critical to contestants for royal power, was not a subject for debate by the general public. There was no forum for the "commoners" who made up the majority of the population to express their opinions; these people were concerned principally with their livelihood. And for this they did not need the weapons that settlers in the wilds of North America came to depend on for their very existence. In England, possession of lethal weapons was a privilege enjoyed largely by the landowning nobility and troops maintained by them and by the ruling monarch, to defend themselves against all challengers—domestic and foreign. Only the military strength of the nobles opposed to a particular monarch gave them the leverage required to demand a share in decisions of public policy.

With the development of parliamentary government, opportunities opened for discussion of public issues by citizens outside the ranks of the nobility and the clergy. But where arms were concerned, the major objective of most commoners was not to make weapons available to all, but to control the monarch's ability to maintain a large standing army that could be used to suppress all opposition. Thus, from the time of the so-called Model Parliament of 1295—whose membership was limited to barons, knights and clergymen—until the Glorious Revolution of 1688, the right to bear arms was not a major issue.

One of the most uncompromising dissertations offered in support of an absolute "individual right to keep arms in the home and to carry them in public" was written for an American audience by Stephen P. Halbrook. Expressing a view dear to the hearts of National Rifle Association officials, Halbrook found in the history of Western civilization countless illustrations of a connection between individual freedom and the private possession of arms.[1] Reviewing some three thousand years of that history, he prefaced his attack on present-day advocates of gun control by attributing to them this view of the problem: "It seems that select military forces, not 'the people,' have a right to keep and bear arms. Even if individuals hold this right, some kinds of arms (such as handguns) are supposedly not really 'arms' at all, and can be banned without infringing on anyone's rights."[2] Having constructed the opposition straw man in this fashion, Halbrook undertakes to demolish it by reference to the writings of philosophers from Plato to John Locke, to the authors of the Second Amendment to the U.S. Constitution, the drafters of the Fourteenth Amendment, and court opinions from the Civil War down to the federal appellate court's 1983 decision in the Morton Grove case.

Despite the multitude of Halbrook's quotations from sages of centuries past, all presumed to support the contention that an unrestricted right to bear arms is essential to a democratic society, a careful reading of these source materials reveals a much narrower message, which is that the individual is always entitled to defend himself against the threat of harm. The broader assumption that an armed public is democracy's best protection rests on the long record of governments ruled by kings, princes or generals whose strict control of arms was to guard against any effort to remove them from power. It does not follow that arming the general public will bring about a democratic society.

Halbrook makes much of Niccolò Machiavelli as a source of inspiration for the Founding Fathers, quoting passages from the Italian writer's "Discourse on the First Ten Books of Titus Livy" to prove Machiavelli's acknowledged preference for a republic over a monarchy. However, early American references to the "Italian Master in politics," as Elbridge Gerry called him, indicate that he was better known for the devious tactics he recommended in a book dedicated "to the most illustrious Lorenzo, son of Piero de' Medici," sixteenth-century rulers of Florence.[3] Halbrook is on firmer ground when he cites Thomas Jefferson as having referred to Aristotle, Cicero, Locke, and Sidney as authors of what Jefferson called "the elementary books of right." However, he then goes on to suggest that Jefferson included the works of a number of other writers in that category, although none of them was mentioned in the letter in which Jefferson used the phrase "elementary books of right" in explaining the background of the Declaration of Independence.[4]

An avid reader of philosophical works, Jefferson was familiar with the writings of every important literary figure from Plato to Adam Smith. He frequently referred to them in his letters and essays, though not always in complimentary terms. The works of Montesquieu, for example, cited as authoritative by Halbrook, Jefferson once described as containing "so much of paradox, of false principle and misapplied fact, as to render its value equivocal on the whole."[5] Machiavelli, on the other hand, is not mentioned once in the 1,690-page collection of Jefferson papers published by the Library of America.

Another expert in paradox, false principle and misapplied fact is former President Ronald Reagan. Fully in sympathy with the views expressed by Halbrook, during his term in the White House, Reagan consistently rejected every proposal for even so simple a requirement as a seven-day waiting period to permit a background check on prospective purchasers of handguns. Only when James A. Brady, his former press secretary who had been critically wounded during the assassination attempt on the president, appeared before a congressional committee to plead for such a measure two years after Reagan had left office, did the latter relent and announce his support for such a law. During his presidency, however, he frequently cited historical examples—never documented—to demonstrate that more severe penalties for crimes committed with guns would be better than restrictions on the possession of guns. During a visit to a Catholic elementary school, one youngster asked the president for his opinion of proposals to limit the sale of weapons. In response, Reagan gave the children a short lecture that included the following statement about British practice in the days before the American Revolution:

In England, if a criminal carried a gun, even though he didn't use it, he was not tried for burglary or theft or whatever he was doing, he was tried for first-degree murder and hung if he was found guilty. They said that the fact that he carried a gun meant that he had premeditated using the gun to kill someone if necessary.[6]

This account of English law and court procedure was, of course, completely false. The facts are quite different. In the "old days" referred to by Reagan, the earliest attempts at policing English streets put emphasis on self-help and included a prohibition against anyone carrying weapons after sundown. A law passed in 1285 provided for the volunteer "watch and ward" societies known to New Englanders centuries later. In 1585 one area of London gave both police and judicial powers to the dean and the high steward of Westminster, who were authorized to punish "all matters of incontinencies, common scolds and common annoyances, and to commit to prison all who offended against the peace."[7] At the time of the American Revolution, London still had unpaid constables and poorly paid night watchmen whose arms and equipment consisted of "rattles, staves and lanterns." A paid Metropolitan Police Force was not established until 1829, when London was described by a police historian as "probably more pre-eminent in crime than any other town in earlier or later history."[8]

During the eighteenth and early nineteenth centuries, it was not uncommon for English thugs to carry weapons—more often knives or clubs than guns. Yet British aversion to the use of any kind of armed force for the maintenance of law and order went back to much earlier days. The force of that tradition was demonstrated during a riotous period in 1830. Placards headed "LIBERTY OR DEATH" were paraded in London streets to warn people that "6,000 cutlasses have been removed from the Tower [of London] for the use of [Prime minister Robert] PEEL'S BLOODY GANG." Asserting that "these damned police are now to be armed," the poster challenged: "Englishmen, will you put up with this?"[9]

A history of that period gives no support whatever to Reagan's assertion that ordinary crimes committed by persons carrying weapons were treated as capital offenses. Regardless of whether or not the alleged criminal was armed, as recently as the early nineteenth century, "a hundred and sixty offenses were recognized as punishable by death." And in no case was the death sentence conditional upon the criminal's possession of a weapon. A former superintendent of Scotland Yard described British criminal law of that era in this fashion:

It is difficult now [in 1936] to realize that in the lifetime of our grandparents a man might be hanged if he appeared in disguise in a public road; if he cut down young trees; if he shot rabbits; if he poached game at night; if he returned to England from transportation [to an overseas penal colony] before the end of his sentence; if, being a Gypsy, he remained in the same place for twelve months. It was even a capital offense to break down the embankment of a fishpond and let the fish escape; to cut down a fruit tree in a garden or orchard; to steal a handkerchief of above the value of one shilling.[10]

In cases like these, only the rabbit hunter or poacher was likely to be armed, and the death sentence prescribed for the hunter was no more terminal than that given the unarmed handkerchief snatcher. Nevertheless, the story Reagan told the schoolchildren lay in his memory bank and was retrieved a few years later when he held a private interview with three *New York Times* newsmen. On that occasion, Reagan offered the tale as an explanation of why British police do not carry guns. His account must have sounded logical to his questioners, as none of them challenged this bit of Reaganesque history.[11] The simplest investigation would have told them that his story had no basis in fact. From the very beginning of London's Metropolitan Police Force, officers were issued weapons only when the lawbreaker was known to be armed and dangerous. The more normal situation was so well understood that in his 1936 350-page history of the origin of Scotland Yard, Sir Basil Thomson devoted only this brief reference to the exception noted above: "It is perhaps worth mentioning here that the only arm carried by the Metropolitan policeman is the truncheon, secured to his wrist by a thong. He carries neither pistol nor handcuffs; these are kept in the police station for use in emergencies."[12]

A more modern chronicle explains that "British police are traditionally not armed with guns" but are taught pistol shooting "simply to enable them to defend themselves when they have to tackle armed criminals." Only officers who guard palaces, "and in times of stress, embassies and the homes of cabinet Ministers, are armed with 9 mm Walthers [pistols]." Even here, the writer says, "one feels that guns are provided more as a reciprocal gesture than as a serious threat to the bomb-thrower." In all other circumstances, he writes, a policeman is issued only a stick, "a heavy piece of turned mahogany" that he "very seldom draws and uses still less often." He may purchase privately a pair of handcuffs, but "few policemen do, since the courts give heavy damages against those who use handcuffs unnecessarily."[13]

If President Reagan's elementary knowledge of history can account for his view of the past and its impact on the future,[14] Stephen Halbrook has no such excuse. His published work indicates that he has researched his subject very thoroughly. But in document after document, he finds a meaning that does not square with the facts. He quotes liberally from English sources, including the laws of ninth-century King Alfred, eleventh-century laws of the legendary King Cnut, the Magna Carta of 1215, and subsequent edicts of British rulers down to the 1689 Bill of Rights. Although his purpose is to prove that all of these statutes demonstrate the British belief in freedom of arms ownership by all people, his quotations clearly show an intent to limit that privilege to property owners, often only to those who had sworn allegiance to the ruling monarch or to his noble followers.

The danger of a government kept in power by maintaining its own army was recognized in England long before the first American colony was established. Queen Elizabeth's one-time favorite, Sir Walter Raleigh, once observed that one of the guiding principles of a tyrant was "to unarm his people and store up their weapons, under pretence of keeping them safe," and then to issue them only to those he could count on to support him in time of trouble.[15] Raleigh's use of the masculine pronoun in referring to the practices of tyrants demonstrates not only his discretion as a servant of Britain's ruling queen, but his knowledge of the way in which monarchs throughout Europe kept themselves in power. A century later, when the British dethroned King James II for his "endeavor to subvert and extirpate the protestant religion and the laws and liberties of the kingdom," Parliament enacted the 1689 Bill of Rights, which included these provisions: "That raising or keeping a standing army within the kingdom in time of peace, unless it be with the consent of Parliament, is against the law. That the subjects which are protestants may have arms for their defence suitable to their conditions and as allowed by law."[16] Halbrook's interpretation of the British Bill of Rights is as flawed as his reading of earlier documents. He assumes that by granting Protestant subjects the right to carry arms "suitable to their conditions," the law broadened that right to include all Protestants as well as previously enfranchised Catholics. This view is refuted by his own later reference to this paragraph in a volume of the *Commentaries* of British jurist William Blackstone, annotated in 1803 by Virginia Judge St. George Tucker:

> In England, the people have been disarmed, generally under the specious pretext of preserving the game. . . . True it is, their bill of rights seems at first view to counteract this policy; but their right of bearing arms *is confined to protestants,* and the words "suitable to their condition or degree" have been interpreted to authorize the *prohibition* of keeping a gun or other engine for the destruction of game, by any farmer, or inferior tradesman, or other person not qualified to kill game. (emphasis added)[17]

As if further evidence were needed to invalidate Halbrook's concept of every Englishman's traditional right to bear arms, he goes on to quote a later edition of the *Commentaries,* published in 1829 by William Rawle, which confirms that under the 1689 Bill of Rights that privilege "was secured to protestant subjects only," and that only "a very small proportion of the people" were licensed to have guns for killing game. "A gun or other instrument used for that purpose by an unqualified person may be seized and forfeited," according to this legal historian.[18]

In one sense, England's age-old tradition in the matter of gun control is irrelevant to practices in colonial America. Eighteenth-century Great Britain was a well-developed, well-organized community, protected against external enemies by surrounding seas and a powerful navy. By comparison, North America was an untapped wilderness which could be conquered only by people having the wherewithal to protect themselves from predators—both human and animal—and to hunt game for food while attempting to raise crops and engage in other pursuits essential to survival in a strange and inhospitable land. In this situation, it is not surprising that arms for self-protection and for hunting were considered a necessity—even an obligation—in colonial America. For that reason, the right to bear arms as a legal question simply did not arise on the North American continent. For as long as the colonies supported the mother country in its recurring wars with other European nations, England was content to see its American settlers enact local legislation requiring all able-bodied men to arm themselves and stand ready to defend their homes and their neighbors against attacks by Indians or by the troops of France, Spain, or any other country that might be at war with England. For the better part of two centuries the colonies did aid the mother country in the conflicts that repeatedly spilled over from Europe to the Americas. These long-drawn-out hostilities included the War of the League of Augsburg, 1689–1697, known to the colonists as King William's War; War of the Austrian Succession, 1702–1713, called in America Queen Anne's War; War of the Spanish Succession, 1740–1748, commonly referred to in the colonies as King George's War; and the Seven Years War, which actually lasted nine years from the first skirmishes in 1754, two years before England formally declared war on France. This last contest, which American residents called the French and Indian War, was the only one to begin in North America, where colonists pushing westward from Virginia, Pennsylvania and New England clashed with French forces that were busy setting up fortified posts throughout the Ohio Valley. The earlier conflicts arose out of political disputes in Europe and spread to the western hemisphere because the two major contenders in each case—Britain and France—were also adversaries in the quest for ever-larger colonial empires. Thus, in more than 170 years of colonization by settlers along the eastern coast of North America, thirty-six years were spent in battles on behalf of the British Crown, albeit in self-defense clashes with Indian tribes, from New England to Georgia and the boundary of Spanish-held Florida.

Throughout this period, the British government was more than willing to have whatever support it could get from the armed settlers who made up the militia of each colony. A change in attitude came with London's growing awareness of the rising tide of resistance to laws passed by Parliament and edicts issued by the king, which the colonists believed were imposed upon them without their having any say in the matter and without regard for the resulting burden placed upon the colonial economy.

Notwithstanding the substantial loss of life and wealth suffered by the colonists, particularly in the French and Indian War, the London government thought it only fair that the colonies bear part of the cost of maintaining continued protection by British troops stationed in America. To recover some of that expense, Parliament levied duties on non-British goods imported into the colonies and added a tax on newspapers, legal documents, and other printed material by means of the hated Stamp Act. To enforce these measures, Parliament added a Quartering Act that required the colonies to provide living quarters and supplies for British troops. Enraged settlers reacted with every means at hand, from formal protests to acts of violence against Stamp Tax agents and other officers of the Crown. Most effective was the boycott of British goods organized by groups of merchants in many of the colonies, a campaign that convinced Parliament to repeal the Stamp Act only a year after its passage. But the seeds of rebellion had been planted and were nourished by repeated demands from Massachusetts to the Carolinas for an end to "taxation without representation."[19]

Whatever concessions Britain was willing to make in matters of trade, on the question of Parliament's right to enact laws enforceable within the colonies, it would not yield. Random acts of violence mounted to armed resistance, which in turn brought ever larger contingents of British troops. Efforts to disarm the rebellious colonists were undertaken, not by legislation but by seizing their stores of weapons and ammunition. In one of these forays, British General Gage sent a thousand troops to commandeer the rebel arsenal at Concord, Massachusetts. Alerted to the plan, the colonists rallied defenders along the route from Lexington to Concord, in the process writing one of the most stirring pages in American history: Paul Revere's ride to warn of the British attack, the gallant stand of seventy patriots on the village green at Lexington, the fierce defense at the Concord bridge that turned back the British troops and the harried retreat of those troops to Boston, in the course of which they lost more than one-fourth of their strength.

Militarily, these were relatively small engagements, but in a very real sense this attempt by Great Britain to impose a form of gun control on the colonies signaled the beginning of the American Revolution.

2

Guns and the Constitution

The revolt of the thirteen colonies was against a system that kept all important political, economic and military decisions in the hands of the government in London, where the welfare of England took precedence over all else. Colonial legislatures were tolerated only as long as they did not challenge the authority of the home government to override their local decisions or to impose laws Parliament thought best for all concerned. When Britain attempted to enforce the more objectionable laws by military means, the colonists considered this a kind of tyranny they were unwilling to accept. They were reminded time and again by leaders like Patrick Henry, James Otis and Samuel Adams that according to many of the original colonial charters, Englishmen in America possessed "all the Liberties, Privileges, Franchises and Immunities that at any Time have been held, enjoyed and possessed by the people of Great Britain."[1]

The notion that British-Americans had the same rights as citizens in the mother country was not limited to the colonists themselves. Stephen Hopkins, British governor of Rhode Island in 1764, described the amalgam of basic concepts from the Magna Carta to the 1689 Bill of Rights as "this glorious constitution, the best that ever existed among men." He also asserted that before the colonists left England, "the terms of their freedom and the relation they should stand in to the mother country in their emigrant state were fully settled: they were to remain subject to the King and dependent on the kingdom of Great Britain. In return they were to receive protection and enjoy all the rights and privileges of freeborn Englishmen."[2]

James Otis had made the same point more forcefully when in 1761 he argued in court that writs of assistance (general, nonspecific search warrants), even if authorized by Parliament, were "against the fundamental principles of [English] law." Anticipating a concept fully and uniquely developed in the United States after independence, Otis declared, "As to acts of Parliament, an act against the constitution is void."[3] What he did not point out was that the 1689 Bill of Rights was no more than a parliamentary statute, which could be repealed or made ineffective by subsequent legislation.

As indicated earlier, even the 1689 Bill of Rights did not confer the right to bear arms on all citizens of Great Britain. In the colonies, however, the need for both protection and sustenance bred a different way of life. Since defense was a community problem as much as it was a matter of personal safety, the concept of an armed militia took hold at an early stage. This was greatly preferred to a standing army, which was viewed as one of the greatest threats to freedom. In fact, the question of militia versus a standing army was under constant discussion during the years of protest against England as well as during later debates over the character of the central government that was proposed for the newly independent United States of America.

Eight years before the Declaration of Independence, Silas Downer, one of the revolutionary Sons of Liberty, delivered a passionate address to a Providence, Rhode Island, audience that included this denunciation of England's use of troops to subdue New England settlers:

A standing army in time of profound peace is quartered about the country to awe and intimidate the people. Men of war and cutters are in every port, to the great distress of trade. In time of war we had no station ships, but were obliged to protect our trade [ourselves], but now in time of peace, when there are none to make us afraid we are visited with a plague of men of war who commit all manner of disorders and irregularities. . . . Unless we exert ourselves in opposition to their plan of subjecting us, we shall all have soldiers quartered about upon us, who will take the absolute command of our families. Sentry boxes will be set up in all the streets and passages, and none of us will be able to pass without being brought to by a soldier with his fixed bayonet, and giving him a satisfactory account of ourselves and business. . . . From which tearful calamities may the GOD of our fathers deliver us![4]

A similar view was expressed by a Protestant minister, Simeon Howard, who described the British-type standing army as "generally composed of men who have no real estate in the dominions which they are to defend; their pay is their living and the main thing that attaches them to their employers." Troops of this type brought in from other parts of the empire, or like the Hessians hired from other countries, he found a threat to liberty. "When there is any difference between rulers and subjects," Howard said, "they will generally be on the side of the former, and ready to assist them in oppressing and enslaving the latter." For the colonies he had this advice:

The keeping up of troops sufficient to guard exposed frontier posts may be proper; but to have an army continually stationed in the midst of a people, in time of peace, is a precarious and dangerous method of security. A safer way, and which has always been esteemed the wisest and best by impartial men, is to have the power of defence in the body of the people, to have a well-regulated and well-disciplined militia. This is placing the sword in hands that will not be likely to betray their trust, and who will have the strongest motives to act their part well, in defence of their country, whenever they shall be called for.[5]

Howard's suggestions, offered in a lengthy sermon to a Boston artillery company in 1773, were merely an extension of past practice, for the settlers had always relied upon themselves for protection. As one military historian explains:

Each of the thirteen colonies, except for Pennsylvania where Quaker influence was dominant, enacted laws providing for a compulsory militia organization, generally based on the principle of the Saxon fyrd that every able-bodied free male from sixteen to sixty should render military service. Each member of the militia was obligated to appear for training at his county or town seat a certain number of days each year, to provide himself with weapons and to hold himself in readiness for call in case of Indian attack or other emergency.[6]

Pennsylvania finally adopted a militia law in 1755, but it made service voluntary rather than compulsory. By that time the Indian threat to settlements along the Atlantic coast had all but disappeared.

As a result, "training days, one a week in the early days of settlement, fell to one a month or even one a year. Festivities rather than military training increasingly became the main purpose of many of the gatherings and the efficiency of the militia in these [coastal] regions declined accordingly." Where volunteer units continued the earlier tradition of taking pride in the distinctive uniforms and public displays they adopted, these became "the predecessors of the National Guard of the United States."[7]

The colonies entered the Revolutionary War completely dependent on an armed population. When called upon by the Continental Congress to prepare constitutions that would replace British law, all thirteen states included, either in their constitutions or early statutes, provisions for establishing and maintaining militia that would be completely under state control. Of the twelve state constitutions written in response to a suggestion circulated by the Continental Congress in May 1776, eleven indicated, directly or indirectly, a need for an armed force—usually specified as the militia—to be raised, "disciplined," and supported by the state. Connecticut was an exception; its brief four-paragraph constitution of 1776 specified a number of protections for the individual's life and property and guaranteed "the same justice" for all "free inhabitants," but in other respects it accepted the royal charter of 1662 as the "civil constitution" of the state. Rhode Island continued to function under the royal charter granted in 1663, supplemented by acts of the state legislature; it did not approve a new constitution until 1842.[8]

On the specific question of the right of individuals to bear arms, only three of the first twelve state constitutions—those of Massachusetts, North Carolina and Pennsylvania—listed this in the "Declaration of Rights" that introduced their constitutions. Rhode Island incorporated such a provision in its 1842 constitution, but by that time many of the newly admitted states had adopted similar provisions, the tendency being to include in state constitutions all of the protections contained in the federal Bill of Rights.

As the war for independence progressed, the realization grew that a more cohesive force than voluntary cooperation among thirteen independent states was needed, particularly if Congress was to be successful in obtaining aid from France, the Netherlands and other old enemies of Great Britain. The first attempt at drafting a constitution began even before the Declaration of Independence. At the suggestion of Richard Henry Lee of Virginia, the

Continental Congress on June 7, 1776, appointed a committee to prepare a document that would join the thirteen states into a confederation. Working with remarkable speed, the committee submitted to Congress on July 12 two alternative drafts of Articles of Confederation.[9]

The Articles finally adopted by Congress contained no bill of rights because, as an editor in the Library of Congress explains, "the rights of individuals were generally believed to be a local matter unrelated to the problem of constructing a confederation between independent states." Hence it is not surprising that Congress "rejected out of hand" a provision in Dickenson's draft that would have guaranteed freedom of religion to all people— men and women alike.[10] Even the widely acclaimed principle of freedom of speech went unmentioned, except for a guarantee of protection for members of Congress against arrest for anything short of "treason, felony, or breach of the peace . . . during the time of their going to and from, and attendance on congress."[11]

On the question of defense, both Bartlett and Dickenson agreed on a provision that would prohibit the maintenance of a peacetime standing army by any state, the only exception being to permit armed men to garrison the forts that had been built in a number of locations, principally along the western frontier. Congress added to this a ban on peacetime "vessels of war," except for those necessary to protect American trade. An attempt by Connecticut to include a provision that "no land army shall be kept up *by the United States* in time of peace" (emphasis added) was voted down, 11 to 1.[12] Each state was expected to maintain "a well regulated and disciplined militia, sufficiently armed and accoutred, and shall provide and constantly have ready for use in public stores a due number of field pieces and tents, and a proper quantity of arms, ammunition and camp equipage." Decisions on war and peace were to be made only by Congress, in which each state had one vote.[13]

Passed by Congress November 15, 1777, the Articles were ratified by most states the following year. But because acceptance of the agreement to establish a "confederation and perpetual union" required the unanimous approval of all thirteen states, it did not go into effect until the last of the thirteen, Maryland, ratified on March 1, 1781. This was less than nine months before the surrender of British General Cornwallis at Yorktown and only twelve months before Britain opened negotiations for a peace treaty. By the time the treaty was signed (September 3, 1783) the Articles had outlived their usefulness. More like a treaty than a constitution, their stipulated intent was to "enter a firm league of friendship" in which "each state retains its sovereignty, freedom, and independence, and every power, jurisdiction and right which is not by this confederation expressly delegated to the United States in Congress assembled." Even a person accused of treason was to be turned over to "the state having jurisdiction of his offence." In short, this was a compact whose principal purpose was to provide for the "common defense" of the signatories.[14]

Even before the Articles became operative, political leaders were pointing out defects in an arrangement that depended on the voluntary cooperation of thirteen separate and independent states. Questions regarding state boundaries were almost as sensitive as those between European rivals for territory in America. On this subject, William C. Houston, a New Jersey delegate to the Continental Congress, complained in March 1780 that "no mode is laid down for deciding between the United States and any one of them as well as between any two or more states where a difference subsists as to boundary."[15] In a letter written July 16, 1780, Philip Schuyler of New York went into far more detail as to the additional powers that should be given the central government, although he still conceived of the Congress as the lone organ of that establishment.[16]

Even as Maryland seemed ready to give the final approval needed to bring the Articles into effect, John Matthews of South Carolina commented to George Washington that "the powers of the confederation are very inadequate to a rigorous prosecution of the present war."[17] A month after the Articles were adopted as the country's first constitution, James Varnum of Rhode Island expressed his despair at the inability of Congress to enforce its decisions regarding state contributions to the war effort. The situation was so serious, he thought, that in a short time Congress would either be "dissolved or laid aside as useless." He went on to suggest a remedy that was not to receive wide support until several years after the war was over. "I know of but one eligible Resort in the Power of the United States," he said.

That is to form a Convention, not composed of Members of Congress, especially those whose political sentiments have become interwoven with their Habits, from a long Train of thinking in the same way. It should be the business of this Convention to revise & refraim [sic] the Articles of

Confederation. To define the aggregate Powers of the United states in Congress assembled, fix the Executive Departments, and ascertain their authorities. Many other matters, subservient to these general ideas would come before them, and their Powers should be extensive in Point of Ratification.[18]

The states' reluctance to accept a central government with the more efficient system of an executive and judiciary separate from Congress was not based on any aversion to the doctrine of separation of powers. They had known such a system through most of their colonial years and had adopted a similar arrangement at the state level shortly after the Continental Congress called upon them in 1776 to set up governments independent of the king. The fear was that a federal executive and judiciary would be given—or would assume—powers that would threaten the sovereignty and independence of the states. This fear was expressed in an accusation later leveled at sponsors of the constitution designed in 1787, that the designers' purpose was to substitute a national government for a federation of independent states, thereby making the states subservient to a powerful central authority.[19]

Equally important was the widespread suspicion that a strong central government might lead to the building of a standing army that could then be used to force state compliance with whatever policies national officials decided upon. This kind of home-grown tyranny was no more attractive than one designed in England, France or Prussia. It was these concerns that provoked demands for two kinds of guarantees during debates in and following the Constitutional Convention of 1787. One was assurance that, except in time of war, the security of the nation would be left in the hands of the state militia rather than to a standing army maintained by the central government. Another was a bill of rights to protect all people from federal encroachment on the individual liberties for which the Revolution had been fought.

The Constitutional Convention opened in Philadelpia May 25, 1787. Notwithstanding the emphasis placed on individual liberty in the protests that had been addressed to King George III, convention members spent almost no time on the subject of a bill of rights. Five days before the convention gave its final assent to the completed constitution, George Mason of Virginia said he wished the plan had been prefaced by a bill of rights. He did not offer a motion to that effect but said he would second such a motion. Elbridge

Gerry of Massachusetts obliged him by moving to set up a committee to prepare a bill of rights. Put to a vote after no more than a few minutes of discussion, the proposal was defeated 10–0, with Massachusetts abstaining and Mason's own Virginia delegation voting against the motion. Roger Sherman of Connecticut expressed the majority view that state protections would not be repealed by the Constitution and a federal bill of rights was therefore unnecessary.[20]

A device that might have given states an opportunity to require that a bill of rights be added before they were asked to consider ratification was suggested by Edmund Randolph of Virginia. On three separate occasions he proposed circulating the draft constitution among the states for their comments and then calling a second convention to consider any amendments the states wished to recommend. Charles Pinckney of South Carolina objected that the states would never agree on the various amendments and a second convention would end in discord, leaving the country with the obviously inadequate Articles of Confederation. Randolph's motion was offered for the third time two days before the convention adjourned, at which point it was rejected unanimously.[21]

The subject of military forces was introduced by George Mason of Virginia on August 18, three-quarters of the way through the proceedings. Mason assumed that the states would be responsible for raising and maintaining their militia, as they had always done; but he felt that for uniformity in their training and discipline, the federal government should be authorized to draw up appropriate regulations. No general discussion ensued at this point, but later in the day the convention reached a provision in the so-called Virginia Plan that would give the national legislature the power to raise armies. Elbridge Gerry of Massachusetts remarked that "there was no check here against standing armies in time of peace." Supported by Luther Martin of Maryland, he proposed that the Constitution stipulate a limit of two or three thousand men for any peacetime army. When this motion was voted down, Mason reverted to his suggestion that Congress be authorized "to make laws for the regulation and discipline of the militia of the several states, reserving to the states the appointment of officers." After several days' discussion, agreement was reached on these points:

The authority to raise and support armies was hedged by a provision that "no appropriation of money to that use shall be for a longer term than two years." Congress was also given authority to "provide and maintain a navy," and to make rules for the regulation of both land and naval forces.[22]

Final disposition of the militia question resulted in these two provisions in what ultimately became a list of the powers of Congress in Article 1, Section 8, of the Constitution:

To provide for calling forth the Militia to execute the Laws of the Union, suppress Insurrections and repel Invasions;
To provide for organizing, arming and disciplining the Militia, and for governing such part of them as may be employed in the service of the United States, reserving to the States respectively, the appointment of the officers and the authority of training the Militia according to the discipline prescribed by Congress.

It is worth noting that in almost every instance, discussion of the militia was linked with references to the danger of maintaining a peacetime standing army.[23] Mason's final effort to amend the previously agreed-upon provisions makes the reason for this clear. He acknowledged that an absolute prohibition against a standing army in peacetime might be unsafe from the standpoint of defense readiness, but as a guard against the tyranny of military rule he urged the convention to preface the clause regarding organization of the militia with the phrase, "And that the liberties of the people may be better secured against the danger of standing armies in times of peace." Although Madison found this compromise acceptable, it was voted down. Only Virginia and Georgia were recorded as favoring the change.[24]

When the finished constitution was submitted to the states for ratification, substantially the same arguments about peacetime armies and militia were heard in almost every state convention. Foremost in the ranks of those whose fear of an overpowerful central government led them to oppose ratification were Virginia's Patrick Henry, Richard Henry Lee and George Mason; Maryland's Luther Martin; Massachusetts Congressman Elbridge Gerry; and New York Governor George Clinton. These men were voicing their opposition even before the first five states to ratify the Constitution did so without attaching any reservations.[25]

Although concern for individual liberty was widely expressed at an earlier stage, it was only after the proposed Constitution had been transmitted to the states for ratification that the absence of a bill of rights became a major issue. It was the subject of debate in Congress as well as in the state ratifying conventions. But the proceedings of Congress were not then open to the public. All the general public knew was that the proposed Constitution was received and read to members of Congress on Thursday, September 20, and was transmitted to the states for ratification on Friday, September 28. However, in that brief interval members of Congress who had little enthusiasm for the plan voiced their objections in no uncertain terms. Edward Carrington, a member of the Virginia delegation who supported the plan, wrote to James Madison warning him that he should not presume his own state's delegation to be solidly behind the proposed system of government. Carrington also confirmed Alexander Hamilton's fear of the substantial opposition brewing among New York representatives.[26]

In Congress the opening gun was fired by Massachusetts delegate Nathan Dane, who observed that the Constitution "appears to be intended as an entire system in itself, and not as any part of, or alteration in the Articles of Confederation."[27] His comments were reported by New York's Melancton Smith, whose notes indicate Dane's belief that "the consolidation is imperfect and will not work. If it does, it will not work on free principles. It must be supported by a standing army. It will oppress the honest and industrious [and] will advantage a few." Smith's notes of the following day's debate reported Richard Henry Lee's attack, which charged: "This plan proposes [to] destroy the Confederation of 13 [states and to] establish a new one of 9." The Articles of Confederation, he said, required any change to be ratified by all thirteen states, while the new Constitution was to go into effect as soon as nine states had approved it.[28]

As Carrington had predicted, Virginia's William Grayson joined in the attack, introducing the problem of a bill of rights, a subject that Richard Henry Lee expanded upon at some length. Nevertheless, when Lee attempted to introduce a number of amendments to the Constitution, to be made before Congress referred it to the states, his motion was defeated. And after a stirring defense of the plan by Madison, Carrington and others, the majority in each state's congressional delegation voted unanimous approval of a motion to transmit the Constitution, unaltered, to the thirteen state legislatures "in order to be submitted to a convention of delegates chosen in each state by the people thereof in conformity to the resolves of the Convention."[29] The Constitutional Convention members' recommendation that the plan be submitted to newly elected delegates to state conventions rather than to the existing state legislatures was prompted by their well-founded fear that too many legislatures might reject it.

Concern for individual liberty under a strict central government was expressed in the state conventions as well as in Congress. Recognizing the intensity of feeling on this subject, James Wilson opened the discussion in the Pennsylvania convention with a lengthy speech strongly supportive of the Constitution, saying he felt "called upon to give a reason why the convention [at Philadelphia] omitted to add a bill of rights to the work before you." His explanation was that the Philadelphia delegates had deliberately designed the new government to be one of delegated powers. Such a government, he said, could not go beyond the powers delegated to it and thereby threaten personal liberty. Thomas McKean, another supporter of the motion for ratification, acknowledged that concern about standing armies and the absence of a bill of rights were two of the major objections voiced by opponents of the Constitution.[30]

Although Pennsylvania was one of the first five states to ratify the unaltered Constitution—along with Delaware, New Jersey, Georgia and Connecticut—once the plan was made public, it became the major topic of conversation and debate throughout the country. As in Congress, criticism was aimed principally at the superior power accorded the national government and the threat this posed to both state sovereignty and individual liberty.[31]

The first serious threat of rejection came when the Massachusetts state convention took up the question of ratification in February 1788. The strength of the opposition is shown by the closeness of the final vote: 187 in favor, 168 opposed.[32] Elbridge Gerry was not a delegate to the state convention, but he requested the privilege of addressing the assembly to express his view of the work of the Philadelphia convention, in which he had taken a very active part. Invited to attend the state convention "to answer any questions of fact that the convention might ask," Gerry was frustrated by not being called upon until ten days after the debates began. The further frustration of being limited to answering specific questions led him to announce that in response to a query regarding the organization of the U.S. Senate, he would prepare a letter that would "set the matter in its true light." The letter Gerry wrote had little to do with the question put to him. Instead, he used the occasion to present all of the reasons why he, along with Edmund Randolph and George Mason, had refused to sign the Constitution.[33]

While Gerry put absence of a bill of rights at the end of his list of objections, George Mason placed it first. Both Massachusetts and Virginia sent with their letters of ratification suggestions for amendments to the Constitution. The Massachusetts recommendations did not include a bill of rights, but in Virginia this led the list of proposed changes.[34] Mason had asked for a bill of rights at the Philadelphia convention, and Patrick Henry returned to this subject time and time again in the Virginia state convention. On almost every occasion he was answered by James Madison.[35]

In most state conventions, delegates who spoke of the individual rights that required protection concentrated on freedom of the press or of religion or trial by jury in civil cases. They seldom mentioned the right to bear arms, as they assumed that if the militia were kept under state control the tradition of bearing arms would be maintained. Thus, when Massachusetts recommended "alterations" in its ratifying message, it made no reference to the right to bear arms. Not until Congress received the ninth ratification, from New Hampshire, did it find among the proposed changes one that coupled a standing army restriction with the statement that "Congress shall never disarm any citizen unless such as are or have been in actual Rebellion."[36] Similarly, when Virginia, New York, North Carolina, and finally Rhode Island ratified, they joined the right to bear arms with their demands for maintenance of state militia in place of a national standing army.[37]

To sum up, five of the thirteen states called for constitutional amendments that would ban a standing army in peacetime and would acknowledge the right of the people to bear arms. Four of those five requested confirmation of the right of states to maintain and control their militia, always relating this to the need for the people to be armed. This, of course, was not the full measure of the demand for a bill of rights. Among the general public there continued to be widespread agitation for amendments that would reinforce the protection of civil liberties. Pressed most vociferously by opponents of the Constitution, the drive for a bill of rights had considerable support from Federalists as well.[38]

The significance of this attitude, particularly as it might threaten the successful establishment of a new national government, was not lost on James Madison. Campaigning for a seat in Congress early in 1789, he pledged his support for amendments that would protect "all essential rights, particularly the rights of conscience, freedom of the press, trials by jury, exemptions from general warrants, etc."[39] Elected to the House of Representatives, Madison spent considerable time collecting, organizing and reducing to their essential elements the many recommendations that had been made during the struggle for ratification of the constitution. On June 8, 1789, he presented the House with a package of amendments that would make the desired changes—not as a separate bill of rights, but by modifying selected clauses in the body of the Constitution.[40]

Although many members of the House agreed that amendments were desirable, the majority felt their energies should be devoted first to the task of designing legislation to organize the new government and to carry out the intent of the Constitution with respect to raising revenue for support of the government, regulating interstate and foreign commerce, and implementing all the other powers assigned to Congress. As a result, Madison's proposal for prompt action on amendments met with considerable resistance. One delay after another forced postponement of his motion until late August. But at that point Madison's perseverance paid off. Had it not been for that persistence, it is unlikely that any action on a bill of rights would have been taken in the first year of government under the Constitution.

Included in Madison's initial list of amendments were these two provisions:

The right of the people to keep and bear arms shall not be infringed; a well armed and well regulated militia being the best security of a free country: but no person religiously scrupulous of bearing arms shall be compelled to render military service in person.

No soldier shall in time of peace be quartered in any house without the consent of the owner; nor at any time but in a manner warranted by law.[41]

These were offered as additions to the specific powers regarding the army, navy and militia given Congress in Article 1 of the Constitution. Notably absent from Madison's package was any suggestion that the power of Congress "to raise and Support armies" be diluted by a ban on a peacetime army.[42]

One aspect of Madison's proposed amendments that is seldom mentioned in discussions of the Bill of Rights is his belief that certain restraints should be placed upon the states as well as the federal government. For this reason he included in his original list of nine amendments one that read: "No state shall violate the equal rights of conscience, or the freedom of the press, or the trial by jury in criminal cases."[43] Although this provision had no direct bearing on the right to bear arms, had it not been eliminated during debate in the House of Representatives, the notion that the Bill of Rights was intended to restrain only the federal government would not have become so firmly fixed in legal tradition. Indeed, the Supreme Court could not have been so uncompromising in its 1833 decision that the first ten amendments "contain no expression indicating an intention to apply them to state governments" and therefore "this court cannot so apply them."[44]

When the House did move on Madison's suggestions, it abandoned the idea of altering the existing articles of the Constitution and adopted seventeen of his recommendations in the form of a bill of rights. The Senate condensed and combined these seventeen into twelve amendments, an arrangement accepted by the House with only minor changes in wording. Ten of the twelve submitted to the states were ratified and became the Bill of Rights that we know today. The second of these ten reads: "A well regulated Militia, being necessary to the security of a free State, the right of the people to keep and bear arms shall not be infringed."

3

The Militia—Then and Now

The importance of the militia as an alternative to a standing army cannot be overemphasized. The long-standing suspicion regarding a standing army as a potential threat to individual liberty did not change with the conclusion of the Revolution. On September 24, 1783, four days after the Treaty of Paris formally ended the war, one military historian wrote, "Congress directed General Washington to discharge 'such parts of the Federal Army now in service as he shall deem proper and expedient.'" Washington followed these instructions, retaining only the force facing British troops that were still in New York. As soon as the British had evacuated that area, the American commander made further cuts, keeping "only one infantry regiment and battalion of artillery, 600 men in all, to guard the military supplies at West Point and other posts."[1]

The inadequacy of such a force, even for protection against internal revolt, became evident during the period when the federal government was struggling to keep the country afloat under the Articles of Confederation. In 1786, an uprising of economically depressed Massachusetts farmers caused Congress to increase the size of the army from 900 to 2,040 men. When this force proved inadequate, the Massachusetts governor called up 5,000 state militia, which brought an end to the threat.

The effect of Shay's Rebellion, as the turmoil in Massachusetts was known, is seen in the reaction of political leaders who were looking for a more stable national government. Even as Congress was considering the suggestion that a convention be called to revise the Articles of Confederation, George Washington wrote to James Madison, "What stronger evidence can be given of the want of energy in our government than these disorders? If there exists not a power to check them, what security has a man for life, liberty, or property?"[2]

Formation of a new and potentially powerful central government in 1789 brought no basic change in the general attitude toward a standing army. Rhode Island's ratification message, which Congress received in 1790 after it had already approved the Second Amendment, included a lengthy statement of support for the militia in place of standing armies, which it declared "in time of peace are dangerous to liberty."[3] Joel Barlow, a prolific writer, political analyst and diplomat, warned in 1792 that "a standing military force is the worst resource that can be found for the defense of a free republic." Still convinced of this in 1801, he wrote:

The more I reflect on the nature of political liberty, the more I am convinced that a military establishment of any magnitude is extremely incompatible with it. The most effectual ways of preventing this, as well the surest mode of providing for the defence of the country, is by a universal attention to arming and disciplining the militia. When every citizen is a soldier, and every soldier will be a citizen, military exercise, to a certain degree, should be considered as a part of education; and though a subordinate part, it should not be neglected.[4]

Congress appeared to hold the same view, making no use of its constitutional authority "to raise and support armies" until, at President Washington's urgent request, it authorized in 1790 an increase in the size of the regular army from 800 men, where it stood in August 1789, to 1,283. But since so tiny a force was inadequate even for protecting the western frontier against Indian attacks, it was assumed, as in the past, that remaining needs would be met by calling up state militia. Until 1792, however, Congress took no action authorized by Article 1, Section 8, of the Constitution "to provide for calling forth the militia to execute the laws of the Union, suppress insurrections and repel invasions." On May 2 of that year it passed the Calling Forth Act, which delegated to the president authority to call up "such number of militia of the state or states most convenient to the place of danger, or scene of action, as he may judge necessary in cases of actual or threatened invasion." In the event of an insurrection, the president was empowered to take the same action if a state legislature or governor requested it. A week later a Uniform Militia Act provided for federal "organizing, arming and disciplining of the militia."[5]

At the close of Washington's eight-year administration, President Adams "inherited [in 1797] a military establishment with an authorized strength of about 3,300 officers and men." Rising tension, first with France, then England, led President Jefferson in 1808 to request a 24,000-man volunteer force. Congress responded by authorizing the "temporary" addition of 6,000 men to protect a nation whose population the 1810 census showed to have grown to 7.2 million. President Madison repeated Jefferson's request in 1810, to no avail. Not until January 1812, five months before the United States declared war on Great Britain, did Congress permit the president to increase the army by 25,700 men. More significant was the further authorization to call up 50,000 militiamen.[6]

The War of 1812 marked a turning point in the general attitude toward a standing army. This is reflected in the following paragraphs from a U.S. military history:

The glory of the victories in the Niagara frontier in 1814 had gone not to the citizen soldier but to the professional. The citizen soldier [militia] properly led, as at the Battle of New Orleans, had on occasion done well; but after the war many military realists questioned the ability of the Army to employ him effectively. There were several reasons. It was extremely hard to obtain from state governments accurate figures on how many militiamen were available. Moreover, the states jealously kept control of arming, disciplining, and training their militia. Though training was crucial, the War Department was limited to making recommendations and supplying training manuals. The Army could not enforce the type of rigorous training that had enabled General Scott to convert Regular soldiers—some of them as raw as militiamen—into the professionals who had excited the admiration even of the British at Chippewa and Lundy's Lane.

As soon as President Madison proclaimed the peace in February 1815, the Congress, forced to meet at Blodgett's Hotel because the Capitol lay in blackened ruins [having been burned by the British], acted promptly to create a small but efficient professional army that was thought adequate—with the addition of the militia—to guard against a repetition of the disasters of the War of 1812. Congress voted a peacetime army of

10,000 men (in addition to the Corps of Engineers), about a third of the actual wartime strength, a figure in marked contrast to the 3,220-man Regular peacetime establishment under President Jefferson.[7]

Contingents of state militia continued to be called upon periodically to assist in wars against the Indians. But when the annexation of Texas in 1845 brought on a war with Mexico, Congress authorized President Polk to augment the peacetime army with 50,000 volunteers rather than call up that many militiamen.[8] Although most of these soldiers were discharged after the war, protection of the enormous territory wrested from Mexico—which included the present states of Arizona, New Mexico, Utah, Nevada and California—led Secretary of War Jefferson Davis to urge expansion of the 10,000-man peacetime army to 27,818.[9]

Six months before Abraham Lincoln's election as president led South Carolina to declare on December 20, 1860, that "the union now subsisting between South Carolina and other States under the name of the 'United States of America' is hereby dissolved," the regular army of the United States had "an actual strength of 1,080 officers and 14,926 enlisted men." Those troops were deployed in seven military departments, or regions, six of which were west of the Mississippi River. The units were so widely scattered that "of 198 line companies, 183 were scattered in 79 isolated posts in the territories. The remaining 15 were garrisoned along the Canadian border and on the Atlantic coast."[10]

Confederate President Jefferson Davis, a West Point graduate who had been the country's secretary of war from 1853 to 1857, did not rely on the militia of the southern states as such, but called for a volunteer army of 100,000 men. Lincoln's initial request to northern state governors for 75,000 militiamen brought pledges of 100,000, which was more than the camps could accommodate. A month later, Lincoln asked Congress for authority to call up volunteers and increase the size of the regular army. Establishing forty new regiments of 42,034 volunteers and adding 22,714 men to the regular army and 18,000 to the navy, he asked state governors to slow the induction of militia. Eventually, close to three million men served in the Union and Confederate armed forces, most of them as volunteers or draftees.[11]

At the conclusion of the war, reductions in military strength were temporarily slowed by the demand for occupation troops in the secessionist states. However, by 1876 the total authorized federal force was down to 27,442, a number that remained virtually stationary until the Spanish-American War in 1898.[12]

This is not to say that the militia fell into disuse. On the contrary, by the end of the nineteenth century Congress had come to recognize that the Militia Act of 1792, which left the organization and training of militia in the hands of the states, could not produce properly prepared and disciplined reserves. Adopting the term National Guard—which some states had already begun calling their militia—Congress in 1903 completely overhauled the century-old legislation, directing that the National Guard be organized and equipped in the same manner as the regular army. Mandated were monthly training periods and annual encampments.[13] In addition, Joel Barlow's notion of military training as part of the educational system bore fruit in the Reserve Officers Training Corps (R.O.T.C.) program. The Morrill Act of 1862, which provided enormous amounts of land to endow state agricultural colleges, included an allowance for military instruction in those institutions. This was the beginning of what was formally organized as the Reserve Officers Training Program in the National Defense Act of 1916.[14]

With the onset of World War I and America's rise to the status of a major world power, debates over the size of the army turned largely on the question of expense. The National Defense Act of 1916 authorized a peacetime army of 175,000 men and a wartime force of 300,000. After the United States entered the war in 1917, restrictions on size disappeared, and before the conflict ended this country had more than 3.6 million men in service.[15]

The war that was to make the world safe for democracy may have failed in that endeavor, but it finally dispelled the notion that a standing army is a threat to personal liberty. Erosion of that concept had begun much earlier, with U.S. visions of expansion at the expense of Mexico ("Remember the Alamo!") and Canada ("54° 40' or fight!"). The Spanish-American War further extended U.S. military commitments into the Caribbean Sea and Pacific Ocean. And after World War I, reductions in the armed forces were dictated by the need to cut expenses rather than fear of military dictatorship.

Completely absorbed into the regular army during World War I, the National Guard subsequently became an important adjunct to the professional military force. In actual numbers, it became "the largest component of the Army of the United States between 1922 and 1939."[16] For all practical purposes, however, the guard had become a formal part of the federal government's military reserve. Available to state authorities in case of extraordinary domestic violence, it was supported, armed and trained largely at federal expense, and was considered to be on call for wartime duty at any time.

The country's later experience merely reinforced that tie. World War II and the subsequent cold war produced a militarized America never conceived by the men who added the Second Amendment to the Constitution. Fourteen years after the close of the Vietnam War, the United States had a peacetime standing army of 772,000 men and women. If Air Force and Marine Corps personnel are included, the on-land or land-based fighting force in 1990 would total more than 1.5 million. The navy's 598,000 men and women bring the total over 2.1 million. In addition, the 1990 federal budget called for National Guard and organized reserves of almost 1.8 million.[17]

A further major change in the conditions for which the Second Amendment was intended is seen in this country's attitude toward its place in the world. In 1789, and for many years thereafter, the American people considered defense needs solely in terms of protection for the homeland—the continental United States. Wars arising out of the conflicts between European powers, which had taken their toll of American lives and wealth throughout the colonial period, were no longer considered the business of America. As President Washington said in that portion of his farewell address that is probably the best known of all his statements:

Europe has a set of primary interests which to us have none or a very remote relation. Hence she must be engaged in frequent controversies, the causes of which are essentially foreign to our concerns. Hence, therefore, it must be unwise in us to implicate ourselves in the ordinary vicissitudes of her politics or the ordinary combinations and collisions of her friendships or enmities.[18]

Tom Paine had made the same point twenty years earlier in his fiery *Common Sense*, the most widely acclaimed revolutionary tract of 1776. His list of "injuries and disadvantages" in continued subservience to Great Britain was more than a call for independence. It reflected the almost universal desire of the colonists to be free of any association that would immerse their country in the politics of any European nation.[19] Even as the Continental

Congress was considering an alliance with France as a means of winning independence from England, John Adams warned: "We ought not to enter any alliance with her which should entangle us in any future wars of Europe; we ought to lay it down as a first principle and maxim of conduct never to be forgotten to maintain an entire neutrality in all future European wars." Years later, when he was engaged in peace negotiations with Britain, he repeated the warning, insisting that "our business with them and theirs with us, is commerce, not politics, much less wars."[20]

Similar sentiments were expressed by Alexander Hamilton, James Madison and John Jay, all of whom had a hand in drafting George Washington's farewell address to the American people. Thus, it was not a new notion that Washington expressed in the most famous of his quoted phrases, in which he advised Americans "to steer clear of permanent alliances with any portion of the foreign world."[21] This was at the core of what later came to be known as isolationism: commercial relations with all, but political entanglements with none.

A modification of that concept evolved in the 1820s when the United States showed its sympathy for Spanish colonists in Latin America who were in revolt against the conquistadors. British Prime Minister George Canning, intent on seeing that France did not take over Spain's tottering empire, suggested joint action by England and the United States to prevent such a development. Secretary of State John Quincy Adams urged President James Monroe to act independently of Great Britain. Monroe did this by including an announcement of U.S. policy in his annual message to Congress. That message, delivered December 2, 1823, contained a lengthy exposition of U.S. attitudes toward colonization on the American continents, referring to Russian-held Alaska in the north and the colonies of Spain and Portugal to the south. The crux of what came to be known as the Monroe Doctrine appeared in this passage:

Our policy in regard to Europe, which was adopted at an early stage of the wars which have so long agitated that quarter of the globe . . . is not to interfere in the internal concerns of any of its powers. . . . But in regard to those [American] continents circumstances are eminently and conspicuously different. It is impossible that the allied powers should extend their political system to any portion of either continent without endangering our peace and happiness.[22]

Revolts by other American colonies against their overlords in Spain, Portugal and France produced in the Monroe Doctrine a corollary to the policy of nonentanglement. If it was in America's interest to keep out of European politics, it was equally important to keep European powers from extending their authority over countries in the western hemisphere. While President Monroe's purpose was to let the revolting colonies go their own way without interference from the United States, on a number of occasions American marines were sent to various Latin American countries, from Cuba to Argentina, to protect U.S. citizens and traders from harm by the revolutionaries and/or pirates who were active from 1822 to the end of the nineteenth century.[23]

One of the most cherished myths of American history is that, with World War I as a temporary aberration, the isolationist policy advocated by George Washington was not truly abandoned until 1941, when the United States entered World War II. In fact, the first indications of a departure from isolationism came not in Europe, as Washington feared, but in the Far East. Led by traders and missionaries, U.S. representatives began pressing Asian governments to guarantee an "open door" to their countries as early as 1842. In that year Commodore Lawrence Kearny negotiated a most-favored-nation trade agreement with the governor of Canton. Two years later, the official Chinese government opened five ports to U.S. traders in the Treaty of Wanghsia.[24]

Unlike commercial treaties with European nations, those with Asian countries usually granted the U.S. (and other Western states) extraterritorial rights. These included the right to maintain military forces in designated areas and to use those forces to protect the commercial privileges guaranteed by the treaties. England had actually gone to war in 1841 to force China to open five of its ports to British trade. The treaty ending that conflict not only accomplished Britain's objective but put Hong Kong entirely in British hands. Three years later, the Treaty of Wanghsia extended the same port privileges to the United States and also exempted Americans from the jurisdiction of the Chinese courts, giving U.S. consular courts authority over both civil and criminal cases involving American citizens.[25]

In actual practice, the United States generally avoided the use of military force, whereas European nations did not hesitate to employ such force when their interests were threatened. Nevertheless, in extending "the same diplomatic protection to its citizens in the Far

East as it did in every other country in the world," the United States took "protective measures" in China that would have been unthinkable in any Western nation. What one historian termed a measure "peculiar to the region" was to put American gunboats on patrol in Chinese rivers and along her coast "as a deterrent to anti-foreign outbreaks."[26] Just how peculiar that was can be judged by considering the explosive response European governments would have had to a U.S. proposal to have its gunboats patrol the Thames River in England, the Seine in France or the Rhine in Germany.

In 1858, after a series of revolts known as the T'ai P'ing Rebellion had been put down by a combination of Chinese, English and French forces, the United States joined Britain, France and Russia in negotiating the Treaties of Tientsin. These opened more Chinese ports to foreign commerce and, at Britain's insistence, legalized the importation of opium, which China had tried to eradicate. Regulations adopted later that year put the Chinese customs service under a British inspector general.[27]

Nearby Japan was opened to Westerners in 1854 by U.S. Commodore Matthew C. Perry. Ten years later, when Japanese "isolationists" attacked a number of foreign compounds and burned the American Legation, the United States, in reprisal, joined European naval forces in the bombardment of Shimonoseki.[28]

In areas of the eastern hemisphere that were less advanced politically and less important in terms of either trading opportunities or size of population, the United States used naval or ground forces to protect American lives, property and commercial shipping on a number of occasions. Between the War of 1812 and World War I, minor military actions were taken 22 times in trouble spots from the Ryukyu Islands in the North Pacific to the Fiji Islands in the South Pacific, and from Korea on the Asian mainland to Sumatra and other islands in the Indian Ocean. These were in addition to 15 forays in China and 4 in Japan. Compared with the 69 military actions taken in Latin America and the Caribbean during the same period, 41 incidents on the far side of the world suggest a substantial "national interest," to use a current phrase.[29]

Notwithstanding the intent of successive American presidents to keep the aim of the U.S. far eastern policy commercial rather than political, America's growing power and expanding interests brought a clear transformation of that policy when, in 1898, this country became embroiled in a war with Spain, a war in which the Spanish-held Philippine Islands became a major target. In taking political control of that Far East territory, historian A. Whitney Griswold says, "American diplomacy departed from the tradi- tions of one century and assumed the obligations of another."[30]

A major impact of this shift in attitude was the demand it placed upon the federal government to maintain a permanent peacetime military force capable of defending not only the homeland and areas covered by the Monroe Doctrine, but American interests halfway around the world. Thus, quite apart from needs generated by formal declarations of war, the determination to maintain on a permanent basis military units capable of protecting Americans everywhere on earth was a further factor in abandonment of the nonentanglement policy so fervently advocated by American political leaders during the early days of the Republic. And with the lapse of that earlier policy, the Second Amendment clause referring to the militia lost its meaning.

Another important factor in the evolution of the arms debate has been the growth of state, municipal and federal police agencies. As indicated in the opening chapter, early American experience was patterned after the self-help system common to cities and towns in Great Britain. Through most of English history, the French origin of the word police "was enough to damn the idea of something like the gendarmerie from the start." The popular notion was expressed by a British historian: "Once admit a police force into England, and the long-cherished liberties of Englishmen would be swept away in a regime of terror and oppression." This view seemed to prevail even after the so-called Gordon Riots, "when for nearly a week in the summer of 1780 London was abandoned to mob violence, from which it was rescued only by the Army, following the personal intervention of the King."[31] Not until passage of the Thames River Police Act in 1800 did London convert a private protection system, initiated by merchants to guard the docks and ships against massive pilferage, into a public police force.[32]

Improvements in the organization and discipline of the London police caught the attention of officials in America, where paid watchmen had replaced many of the voluntary "watch and ward" groups. Unlike their British counterparts, American police, even in these early years, were armed. However, as one chronicler explains, "they wore no uniforms and bore no resemblance to the militia." The adoption of uniforms to enhance the dignity and discipline of police forces in most American cities did not raise their popularity. As in England, distrust of what was conceived as the "police mentality" was deeply rooted and was not softened by the fact that many of those recruited for police duty were of questionable moral character.[33]

By the mid-nineteenth century, every American city and town of any importance had its paid police force. And early in the twentieth century a national police was organized under the U.S. Department of Justice. When that department was first created in 1870, it had only federal marshals to search for and arrest people charged with federal crimes. These officers, like the federal attorneys they worked under, "were political appointees with little or no law-enforcement experience."[34] Subsequent reliance on agents borrowed from the Customs Bureau and Treasury Department were abandoned in 1908 when the Justice Department organized its own Bureau of Investigation. This unit grew rapidly during World War I when problems of espionage and subversion were added to its normal duties of enforcing national laws relating to banking, antitrust actions and offenses against government officials or property.[35] The bureau's further development, after J. Edgar Hoover was appointed director in 1924 by Attorney General Harlan Fiske Stone, is an oft-told story.

The more recent growth of federal enforcement agencies, including the FBI, Secret Service, Customs Service, Immigration and Naturalization Service, and later additions like the Drug Enforcement Administration, has been phenomenal. But for most Americans it still has less personal impact than the thousands of local police forces that are the principal source of protection for the nation's cities, towns and countryside. And it is at this local level that the battle for gun control has been fought most vigorously.

Neither the proliferation of law enforcement agencies nor the change in attitude toward a standing army has altered the opinion of some Americans that the Second Amendment prevents the government from interfering with their right to bear arms. On the contrary, under the aggressive leadership of President Ronald Reagan, many of his supporters came to believe that their country was truly what Reagan called "the last best hope of man on earth,"[36] and that to retain that preeminent position it must build a military machine second to none. The most enthusiastic supporters of that view were also the most avid defenders of the right of every individual to bear arms. But neither President Reagan nor the gun lobby acknowledged the effect of the substantial change in conditions that had occurred since 1776, when an armed civilian population was essential to the defense of the new nation. As Supreme Court Justice Sandra Day O'Connor wrote about the court's responsibility in deciding whether or not to reverse an earlier decision, a major factor to consider is "whether facts have so changed or come to be seen so differently, as to have robbed the old rule of significant application or justification."[37]

4

Guns and the Law

History

A people in revolt against tyranny must arm themselves if they are to have any hope of freeing themselves from the tyrants who rule over them and of maintaining that freedom thereafter. Colonial America, unlike the country that controlled her, was not burdened by laws restricting private ownership of weapons. Except for wartime emergencies involving the mother country, each colony relied for its protection on local laws that required every able-bodied male to arm himself and stand ready to assist in the colony's defense when called upon to do so.[1] This satisfied the mother country, for in England's periodic wars with her colonizing competitors—chiefly France—she expected the colonists to contribute to their own defense. And contribute they did, as indicated in earlier chapters. Thus it was an armed people who led the revolt against England in 1776. And to ensure their continued freedom, the citizens of the new United States of America saw to it that no legal barriers were erected to prevent them from retaining the arms that had helped win their freedom.

The principle of the "armed people" was established in laws that designated the militia as the chief source of defense, not only of each state, but of the nation as a whole. A few states, like Virginia, New York, New Hampshire and Rhode Island, incorporated this principle into their constitutions, along with warnings against the danger of a standing army under the control of the national government. Even Pennsylvania, which had a large pacifist Quaker population, required every able-bodied male to take part in the defense of the community, although its constitution guaranteed that any man "conscientiously scrupulous of bearing arms" could not be compelled to join the militia if he would pay someone else to serve in his place.[2] Some states, like Vermont—the first to enter the Union after independence—emulated Pennsylvania by writing into the constitution an explanation that each citizen was entitled to the state's protection but was also obligated to "contribute his proportion towards the expense of that protection and yield his personal service when necessary, or an equivalent thereto."[3] The equivalent was usually, as in Pennsylvania, payment to another person to take the payer's place in the ranks.

Apart from constitutional provisions, statutory law had long required militiamen to purchase and maintain their own weapons. During the early years before and after independence, when Indian attacks were still a threat everywhere but on the well-settled Atlantic coast, some states required not only that the men of the community arm themselves but that they carry their weapons with them in their travels. An act passed by the Georgia legislature in 1770 mandated "every male white inhabitant of this province . . . who is or shall be liable to bear arms in the militia . . . and resorting . . . to any church . . . shall carry with him a gun or pair of pistols" and shall "take the said gun or pistols with him to the pew or seat."[4]

Widespread aversion to standing armies—whether federal or state—induced delegates in many of the first state constitutional conventions to couple a provision that "no standing army shall be kept up without the consent of the legislature" with one asserting that because a well-disciplined militia is essential to the security of the state, "the right of the people to bear arms shall not be infringed." Where this was done, the state constitution became the controlling instrument. Elsewhere, as in the original (1776) Maryland constitution, the fundamental law provided for a militia without any direct reference to the individual's right to bear arms. In that case, one anti-gun-control writer declares, "the militia clause guaranteed the right of the people at large to keep and bear arms."[5] Even if neither militia nor an arms guarantee was included in a state's bill of rights—which was true of the first Delaware constitution—this writer asserts that "the defacto right of the citizen to bear arms went unchallenged."[6] Certainly that was true for many years after the Revolutionary War. It was recognized by the authors of the federal Constitution as well, including those who saw no need to include a statement to that effect in the fundamental law of the land. Even James Madison, who fought as hard as anyone for adoption of a constitution that would establish a strong central government, accepted the armed-people doctrine in one of the essays he wrote in the *Federalist* papers. Assuming the unlikelihood that those in the national government might betray their trust by pursuing "some fixed plan for the extension of the military establishment," Madison wrote:

State governments, with the people on their side, would be able to repel the danger. The highest number to which, according to the best computation, a standing army can be carried in any country, does not exceed one hundredth part of the whole number of souls; or one twenty-fifth part of the number able to bear arms. This proposition would not yield, in the United States, an army of more than twenty-five to thirty thousand men. To these would be opposed a militia amounting to near a half a million citizens with arms in their hands, officered by men chosen from among themselves, fighting for their common liberties, and united and conducted by state governments possessing their affections and confidence. It may well be doubted whether a militia thus circumstanced could ever be conquered by such a proportion of regular troops. Those who are best acquainted with the last successful resistance of this country against British arms, will be most inclined to deny the possibility of it.[7]

As indicated earlier, most of Madison's colleagues in the Constitutional Convention believed there was no need to include this principle in the written constitution. But in deference to the fears of many members of the state conventions, he almost single-handedly designed and pushed through the first Congress a bill of rights that included the Second Amendment.

As new states entered the Union, the tendency of their constitution writers was to include a bill of rights—or "Declaration of Rights"—at the very beginning of the document. These sections were, in general, patterned after the first ten amendments that had been added to the federal constitution, although not all included the right to bear arms. No reference to that subject was contained in the original constitutions of California, Iowa, Minnesota and Nebraska. However, many went beyond the list of federal guarantees. Some states introduced new provisions as their constitutions were revised, either by conventions or other amendment processes. Maryland's most recent constitution, prepared in convention in 1867, contains a Declaration of Rights forty-six paragraphs in length. In addition to the commonly accepted conditions, it bans poll taxes and monopolies and establishes the principle that rotation in executive offices "is one of the best securities of permanent freedom."[8]

States like Alaska and Hawaii tailored their constitutions to the special circumstances of those areas. Alaska's native population is protected by a provision in which the state disclaims any right or title to property "held by or for any Indian, Eskimo, or Aleut." Similarly, Hawaii's multiracial society, which is largely nonwhite, has included several clauses that recognize that condition. One mandates that "the state shall promote the study of Hawaiian culture, history and language." Another makes both Hawaiian and English the official languages of the state. A third protects the "traditional and cultural rights [of] descendants of native Hawaiians who inhabited the Hawaiian Islands prior to 1778" when the islands were "discovered" by British captain James Cook.[9]

All states have used the amendment process to make limited changes in their constitutions, and most have used a convention when a major overhaul of the system was deemed necessary. Louisiana, which entered the Union in 1812, has held ten conventions, the most recent in 1975. Massachusetts, on the other hand, has not called a convention since its first such gathering in 1780. That New England state's fundamental law was originally designed to ensure complete freedom in decisions affecting the state's defense. In a section subsequently revised was a statement that the governor "for the time being shall be commander-in-chief of the army and navy, and of all the military forces of the state." This paragraph went on at some length to describe the chief executive's almost unlimited power to put the military "in a warlike posture," and to

pursue, by force of arms as well by sea as by land, within and without the limits of the commonwealth; and also to kill, slay, and destroy, if necessary, and conquer, by all fitting ways, enterprises, and means whatsoever, all and every such person ... as shall ... in a hostile manner, attempt or enterprise the destruction, invasion, detriment, or annoyance of this commonwealth.[10]

Although the import of constitutional guarantees of the right to bear arms is the same everywhere, there are significant variations in wording from state to state. Most refer to the right of "the people," but many specify "citizens" as beneficiaries of this right. Prior to the Civil War, the term "citizen" excluded slaves and the thousands of indentured servants who had been brought from other countries under contracts that bound them to their employers for a specific term of years. In the principal slave-holding states it was not uncommon for the phrase "free white men" to be used in identifying those entitled to bear arms and obligated to serve in the militia. Arkansas, in 1836, and Florida, in 1838, incorporated such a provision in their constitutions.[11]

Most often the purpose of the arms clause is explained by the phrase, "for the defense of themselves and the state." Several states, led by Mississippi, expanded the defense to include "home, person, or property, or in aid of the civil power," that is, when called to duty in the militia. Nevada introduced the hunting theme in its statement that every citizen is entitled to bear arms "for security and defense, for lawful hunting and recreational use and for other [unspecified] lawful purposes."

The inventive minds that in the country's first century of freedom produced so many new products and new ways of doing things brought advances not only in the design of industrial equipment but in that of guns as well. Eli Whitney, inventor of the cotton gin, turned to arms production in 1798, and to satisfy his major customer, the U.S. government, he developed a method of making identical rifle parts that could be interchanged or substituted in case of damage. Simeon North had the same success with interchangeable pistol parts. In 1835 the single-shot pistol was outdated by Samuel Colt's design of a hand gun with a revolving cylinder capable of holding five or six bullets. Oliver F. Winchester introduced his repeating rifle the year the Civil War began, and two years later Richard J. Gatling used Colt's revolving cylinder concept to produce the first machine gun. Another war produced a less bulky rapid-fire weapon, when in 1916 John T. Thompson devised what came to be known as a submachine gun. Subsequent refinements appeared during and after World War II, when military needs produced—in many different countries—a variety of weapons now referred to as assault rifles.

All through this period, restrictions on personal ownership and/or use of guns were slow to develop. In the early years of the Republic, carrying arms in public was a common and accepted practice. But some uses of those weapons were forbidden. To terrorize others, for example, or to intimidate a judge or jury in a court of law was punishable by imprisonment and confiscation of the weapons.[12] Dueling as a method of settling private disputes was also proscribed in many states, beginning in New Jersey, where in 1804 Alexander Hamilton was killed by Aaron Burr. This did not discourage such inveterate duelers as Andrew Jackson, who capped a career in such activities with an 1817 challenge to Winfield Scott, who declined to participate "on religious grounds."[13]

Had Jackson died in such an encounter, the country would undoubtedly have seen a very different kind of president during the years 1829–1837 when, in fact, Jackson occupied that post. Scott's death would have deprived the nation of a military commander whose exploits during the War of 1812 and the Mexican War helped make him the Whig party candidate for president in 1852. But that party would probably have met the same defeat Scott suffered if it had chosen to support Millard Fillmore, who had succeeded to the presidency on the death of Zachary Taylor.

As an earlier study points out, most of the restrictions imposed on the state level during the nineteenth century did not prohibit gun ownership. Rather, they were aimed at the ways in which weapons might be handled. Prohibition against the carrying of concealed weapons was one of the earliest to gain general acceptance. Kentucky passed such a law in 1813, and states in other parts of the country—Arkansas, Georgia and Indiana—adopted similar measures shortly after.[14] Colorado's 1876 constitution listed the right to bear arms in its bill of rights but stipulated that this did not include concealed weapons. Florida and Georgia broadened this reservation by amending their fundamental laws to provide that although the right of the people to bear arms shall not be infringed, "the manner of bearing arms may be regulated by law."[15] In 1970 Illinois went a step further, modifying its bill of rights in a fashion that paved the way for municipalities to design local restrictions. Section 22 of the Illinois bill of rights now reads: "*Subject only to the police power*, the right of the individual citizen to keep and bear arms shall not be infringed" (emphasis added). It is under the police power that most state and local regulations have been promulgated.

Important as constitutional guarantees may be, their effectiveness depends in large measure on the way in which they are implemented by statutes, ordinances and administrative regulations. The wide variety of state laws currently applied to the use of guns can be found in the U.S. Treasury Department's 1994 publication, *State Laws and Published Ordinances—Firearms*. Not all local ordinances are included in that report. For example, the prohibition against the discharge of a weapon within town or city limits, in public places or on private property, is so universally applied as to need no documentation. However, those sections of each state's laws that deal with questions of manufacture, sale, possession and transportation of firearms are reproduced just as they appear in the official statutes. Also included are city and town ordinances that establish more stringent controls than those found in state law, as well as statutory provisions that in some states prohibit local authorities from enacting any gun-control measures. Table 4.1 summarizes the various kinds of regulations found in the laws of the fifty states, the District of Columbia and U.S. overseas territories.

A few of the more common characteristics are worth noting. Notwithstanding the great to-do over a federal law to impose a waiting period on purchases of handguns, by 1989 this type of regulation had been adopted by twenty states plus the District of Columbia and the territories of Samoa and the Virgin Islands.[16] The duration of the waiting period varies widely from state to state, ranging from 24 hours for long guns in Illinois to a maximum of six months for a pistol in New York. There are also differences in application. Most states apply a waiting period to handgun buyers only, but a few make it a requirement for the purchase of any firearm. This is true in Hawaii, Illinois and Pennsylvania. Alabama's 48-hour wait applies to any pistol purchase, while Washington's 60-day delay affects only nonresident purchasers of handguns. Other states in which out-of-state buyers must wait longer than state residents include New Jersey, where the delay is 30 days for residents and 45 days for others, and Virginia, where the difference is from one day to 10 days. Connecticut imposes a two-week wait on handgun purchases, but once an individual has obtained a permit for such a weapon, no wait is necessary. In Pennsylvania, once a permit has been granted the holder may buy as many weapons as desired, including handguns. Some thirty states have no waiting period. While the great majority of these are in the West and South, this group also includes Delaware, Maine, Massachusetts, Michigan, New Hampshire, Ohio and Vermont.[17]

Table 4.1
Certain Elements of State Laws, 1994

STATE (OR OTHER) NAME	STATE-PURCHASER WAITING PERIOD	STATE-LICENSE: DEALER, MANUFACTURER, ETC.	STATE-LOCAL GOV'T LIMITS (PREEMPTION)	BRADY STATES (FEDERAL 5-DAY WAITING PERIOD?)
ALABAMA	13-A-11-77; 48 hrs; pistol	13-A-11-78	11-45-1.1	YES
ALASKA			29.35.145	YES
AMERICAN SAMOA	46.4221, .4229 Any firearm; time n/a	46.4223		NA
ARIZONA			13-3108	YES*
ARKANSAS			14-16-504	YES*
CALIFORNIA	12071, .072; 15 days. Concealable	12070; 12292; 12305	(12071(a))	NO
COLORADO	Instant check			NO
CONNECTICUT	29-33 Handguns-None with permits; 2 weeks without 29-37f-Rifles, shotguns-2 weeks	29-28-Pistols & revolvers		NO
DELAWARE		24-901	Title 9, 330(c)	NO
DISTRICT OF COLUMBIA	22-3204; 48 hrs; Pistol	6-2341(b); 22-3209,-3210	NA	NA
FLORIDA			790.33	NO
GEORGIA				YES*
GUAM		60104, 60115		NO
HAWAII	134-2(e); Up to 16 days.	134-31		NO
IDAHO			31-872; 50-343	YES*
ILLINOIS	720 ILCS 5/24-3(g): 72 hours. concealable; 24 hrs. longguns		430 ILCS; (5)/73.1)	NO
INDIANA	35-47-2-9(c)-11 7 work days; handguns	35-47-2-15	35-47-2-13	NO
IOWA	724.15; Application annual permit 724.20; Validity - 3 days after approved date up to one year		724.28	NO
KANSAS				YES
KENTUCKY			65.870	YES
LOUISIANA			40:1787; 47:382, .383	YES*
MAINE			Title 25, § 2011	YES*
MARYLAND	442(b); 481E(b)(2) 7 days. Handguns & Assault Weapons	443	36H: Note # 406; 442(d); 445(a)	NO
MASSACHUSETTS		140:122, 122B		NO
MICHIGAN				NO
MINNESOTA	624.7132(4); Pistol, 5 days		471.633	NO
MISSISSIPPI				YES*
MISSOURI	571.090.3: Concealable; not to exceed 7 working days		21.750	NO
MONTANA			45-8-351	YES
NEBRASKA	69-2418: Instant check by 1995		69-2404	NO
NEVADA				YES
NEW HAMPSHIRE		159:8		YES
NEW JERSEY	2C:58-3 F: Handgun; Resident: 30 days; Others, 45 days	2C:58-1, -3	2C:1-5.6	NO
NEW MEXICO				YES
NEW YORK		400.00.2	400.00.6	NO
NORTH CAROLINA	14-404, -409.3; Pistol, Up to 30 days	14-402, -409.1, 105-80, -102.4	(105-80(c))	YES*
NORTH DAKOTA		2209-2210-2217	62.1-01-03	YES*
COMMONWEALTH OF THE NORTHERN MARIANAS			2227	YES*
OHIO				YES
OKLAHOMA	166.420(5)(A) - Handguns-15 days.		1289.24	YES

44

STATE (OR OTHER) NAME	STATE-PURCHASER WAITING PERIOD	STATE-LICENSE: DEALER, MANUFACTURER, ETC.	STATE-LOCAL GOV'T LIMITS (PREEMPTION)	BRADY STATES (FEDERAL 5-DAY WAITING PERIOD?)
OREGON			166.245	NO
PENNSYLVANIA	6111(a)Any firearm	6112,6113	6120(a)	YES*
PUERTO RICO		432-434	-	YES
RHODE ISLAND	11-47-35(A) Pistols/Revolvers	11-47-38	11-47-58	YES*
SOUTH CAROLINA		23-31-130..-150	23-31-510	YES*
SOUTH DAKOTA	23-7-9:With valid permit to carry - no waiting. With no permit - 48 hrs.		7-18A-36; 8-5-13; 9-19-20	YES*
TENNESSEE			39-17-1314	NO
TEXAS			215.001	YES
UTAH			76-10-501(1)(6B)	NO
VERMONT			Title 24 § 2295	YES
VIRGINIA	18.2-308.2:2	15.1-§23,525	15.1-29.15	NO
VIRGIN ISLANDS	466Waiting period of	461,462		NO
WASHINGTON	9.41.090	9.41.110	9.41.110(7); 9.41.290; 9.41.300	NO
WEST VIRGINIA			8-12-5; 8-12-5a	YES*
WISCONSIN	175.35:Handguns waiting period 48 hrs.	941.25		YES*
WYOMING			-	YES

FOOTNOTES

[Any section citation indicated above should be reviewed for ACTUAL impact.]

1. "STATE" includes the 50 States; the District of Columbia (DC); American Samoa (AS); Guam (GU); Northern Marianas (MP), a Commonwealth; Puerto Rico (PR), a Commonwealth; Virgin Islands (VI).

2. "STATE - PURCHASER WAITING PERIOD" generally refers to the period between purchaser application for firearms and allowable receipt or delivery. Exceptions exist among the States.

3. "STATE- LICENSE: DEALER, MANUFACTURER, ETC." generally means the person must have BOTH a Federal and State license.

4. "STATE- LICENSEE RECORDKEEPING REQUIREMENTS" this category may refer to relatively narrow types of firearms or situations.

5. "STATE- LOCAL GOVERNMENT LIMITS (PREEMPTION)" means that the State overrides its counties, cities, and/or other local jurisdictions, in whole or in part. Entries in parenthesis { ( ) } indicate that permission of some type is specifically GRANTED to local jurisdictions to enact local ordinances.

* Legislation pending to qualify as an "alternate State".
** In these States, the Federal 5-day waiting period does not apply to transfers of handguns to persons holding valid permits/licenses to carry handguns issued within 5 years of the proposed purchase.

DRAFTING INFORMATION

OFFICIAL INTERPRETATION of any State or local law must be left to officials of the relevant jurisdiction(s).

Materials, advice and information for future editions may be addressed to:

BUREAU OF ALCOHOL, TOBACCO AND FIREARMS
FIREARMS and EXPLOSIVES DIVISION
650 Massachusetts Avenue, NW
Washington, DC 20226

Table 4.1 (continued)

BRADY LAW

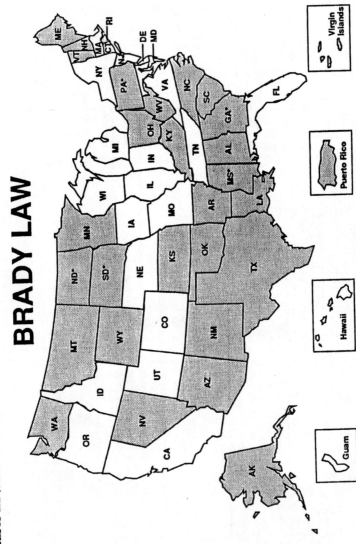

States which must comply with the Federal requirements.

States which meet the Federal requirements through an alternative.

NOTE: * Federal 5-day waiting period does not apply to persons with valid permits/licenses to carry handguns issued within 5 years.

The requirement of a permit before purchase is another common element in state law, although the only application of this rule by all fifty states concerns requests to carry a concealed weapon. Otherwise, the most frequent use of a permit is to identify the weapon and the purchaser and seller of a handgun.

About half of the states also license firearms dealers. The remainder either don't feel this to be necessary or are content to leave that problem to the federal government, whose control is based on its authority over interstate commerce.

The basic federal statute reads as follows:

It shall be unlawful—

(1) For any person, except a licensed importer, licensed manufacturer, or licensed dealer, to engage in the business of importing, manufacturing, or dealing in firearms or ammunition, or in the course of such business to ship, transport, or receive any firearm or ammunition in interstate or foreign commerce.[18]

What the federal Bureau of Alcohol, Tobacco and Firearms (BATF) calls "purchaser requirements" can be found in most state laws. Commonly, whether or not a permit or waiting period is mandated, a purchaser must fill out a form—provided by the seller—giving his name, address and age, and often such additional information as occupation, sex, race and physical description. Twenty of the states that mandate some kind of record keeping dispense with both permits and waiting periods. Most of these states, and a few others as well, have no licensing law for either dealers or manufacturers.

Over the years, both state and national legislatures have decided that some types of weapons are most dangerous in civilian hands and should therefore be subject to some sort of control. As far back as the late 1920s and early 1930s the machine gun was considered a weapon of mass destruction used principally by criminals. For that reason the National Firearms Act of 1934 attempted to curtail commerce in machine guns, sawed-off shotguns, silencers and other "gangster-type" weapons.[19] The act was broadened to include additional arms and ammunition in the Federal Firearms Act of 1938 but, as one study puts it, the act was "a symbolic denunciation of firearms in the hands of criminals, coupled with an inexpensive and ineffective regulatory scheme that did not inconvenience the American firearms industry or its customers."[20]

Another thirty years were to pass before Congress was induced by rising public pressure to strengthen federal controls over the trade in firearms. In the interim, some states enacted their own legislation to put machine guns and dangerous explosives on the forbidden list. They were further encouraged in that direction by passage of the federal Gun Control Act of 1968. In approving this law Congress took pains to mollify gun owners and manufacturers by its explanation of purpose in the following introduction:

Congress hereby declares that the purpose of this title is to provide support to Federal, State, and local law enforcement officials in their fight against crime and violence, and it is not the purpose of this title to place any undue or unnecessary Federal restrictions or burdens on law-abiding citizens with respect to the acquisition, possession, or use of firearms appropriate to the purpose of hunting, trapshooting, target shooting, personal protection, or any other lawful activity, and that this title is not intended to discourage or eliminate the private ownership or use of firearms by law-abiding citizens for lawful purposes, or provide for the imposition of Federal regulations of any procedures or requirements other than those reasonably necessary to implement and effectuate the provisions of this title.[21]

Nevertheless, the law did establish the principle that "no person shall engage in business as a firearms or ammunition importer, manufacturer, or dealer until he has filed an application with, and received a license to do so from, the Secretary [of the Treasury]." Further, restrictions were placed on sales to felons, fugitives from justice, drug addicts and mental defectives. Interstate transportation of machine guns and short-barreled rifles and shotguns was made subject to authorization by the Treasury Department, and except for weapons shipped to military or security personnel, the law declared that "pistols, revolvers, and other firearms capable of being concealed on the person are nonmailable."[22]

More recently, automatic and semiautomatic rifles and pistols designed for military combat, commonly referred to as assault weapons, have come in for special attention due to their devastating effect in the massacres of civilians, which has been demonstrated on a number of occasions. As a later chapter will reveal, anticontrol forces have succeeded in preventing, or at least delaying, the passage of laws, at both federal and state levels, aimed specifically at this type of weapon. Nevertheless, some progress has been made in this direction. Moreover, the basis for control already exists in both federal and many state laws. This is found in restrictions on possession of machine guns, which are included in listings of what many states define as "prohibited weapons." The usual definition of a machine gun is a firearm that shoots automatically a number of shots "without manual reloading, by a single function [pull] of the trigger." This is the same definition that was included in the federal Gun Control Act of 1968.

Other devices that are normally subjected to some kind of state control are explosive weapons—referred to as "infernal machines" in Mormon Utah—as well as sawed-off shotguns and rifles, armor-piercing ammunition and silencers. In some jurisdictions the list is extended to include bombs, grenades, rockets, mines and similar types of explosives. All of these are presumed to be intended for illicit purposes when held by private persons. In most states they are identified as "prohibited weapons."

Under definitions provided in many state statutes, assault rifles would qualify as machine guns, even though they are not treated as such in most jurisdictions. But because these military-type weapons have figured so prominently in mass murders and gang wars, a few states have felt it necessary to make specific reference to assault weapons in their gun-control laws. In the face of bitter opposition from the National Rifle Association (NRA) and some powerful individuals like former President Reagan and then-President Bush, California acted in 1989 to restrict the sale and possession of this type of rifle "based upon the finding that each firearm has such a high rate of fire and capacity for firepower that its function as a legitimate sports or recreational firearm is substantially outweighed by the danger that it can be used to kill and injure human beings." As to the claim that such weapons are appropriate for hunting, Maine disposed of that fiction when it wrote into its conservation laws a prohibition on the use by hunters of all automatic firearms or auto-loading firearms having a magazine capacity of more than five cartridges.

Even President Bush acknowledged that sportsmen do not require "those 30-round magazines" in their hunting weapons. Addressing a group of law enforcement officers in 1989, he reminded them that he had instructed BATF to suspend the importation of certain assault weapons, adding these remarks:

[B]ATF is continuing its examination to determine which, if any, of these weapons are not acceptable under the standards in existing law. And the standard talks about suitability for sporting purposes—and you're hearing this from one who prides himself on being a sportsman, and have been a hunter all my life. And at the conclusion of this study, and after careful consideration, we will permanently ban any imports that don't measure up to these standards. I am going to stand up for the police officers in this country.

And toward this end, I am proposing the prohibition of the importation *and manufacture* of gun magazines of more than 15 rounds for citizens' use. I just don't believe that sportsmen require these 30-round magazines if the legitimate purpose is sports (emphasis added).[23]

If, in fact, he made such a proposal, it never appeared in any of the crime control bills he sent to Congress. Rather, those bills focused on increasing the penalties for criminal use of weapons. And in that area Bush failed to carry his own reasoning to its logical conclusion. As a prelude to the remarks just quoted, he said, "I call on Congress to do for dangerous firearms what it has wisely done for dangerous drugs. I propose to double the mandatory penalties for the use of semi-automatic weapons in crimes involving violence or drugs."[24] What he neglected to point out was that what Congress had wisely done for dangerous drugs was to prohibit their sale to anyone except individuals whose need for a particular drug had been certified by a licensed physician. Had he thought about this aspect of the problem, he probably would not have chosen the example he did, as the obvious question it raises is why the sale of dangerous weapons, like the sale of dangerous drugs, should not be restricted to those whose need has been verified by competent authority.

Bush's successor in the White House, Bill Clinton, took a very different view of the situation. Questioned about the problem of violence in the schools, he said the United States was "the only country I know of where we would permit children access to weapons that make them better armed than police forces." He took that occasion to express his unqualified support for the Brady bill, which passed a short time later, and a bill "which would ban assault weapons."[25]

Not all states permit their municipalities to legislate on the subject of gun control. At this writing, fourteen states assume preemptive control of all regulations concerning the manufacture, sale, licensing, registration, transportation and distribution of weapons. This exclusive assumption of authority is generally expressed in a section of the statutes entitled "State Preemption," as in Rhode Island, or in a section that sets limits on the actions municipalities may take.

A sample of what is known as the "preemption" clause is found in this portion of Oklahoma law:

The State Legislature hereby occupies and preempts the entire field of legislation in this state touching in any way firearms, components, ammunition and supplies to the complete exclusion of any order, ordinance, or regulation by any municipality or other political subdivision of this state. Any existing or future orders, ordinances or regulations in this field except as provided for in subsection C of this section are null and void.

The exceptions are ordinances relating to the discharge of firearms within the jurisdiction of a municipality and those which conform "exactly, except for penalty provisions," with state law. The state's principal restrictions concern sales to minors or convicted felons and possession of sawed-off shotguns and rifles and armor-piercing bullets.

The preemption clause is also used in jurisdictions that wish to ensure statewide compliance with more strict regulation of firearms. New Jersey, for example, forbids its local governmental units from enacting or enforcing "any ordinance or other law or regulation conflicting with, or preempted by any provision in this [state criminal] code." Following this preliminary statement is a lengthy description of the many controls the state has established over the manufacture, sale, possession and transportation of firearms.

Resistance to gun control is sometimes a reflection of regional or cultural influences. The Arizona constitution recognizes the danger of "vigilante justice" by hedging its arms guarantee with the reservation that "nothing in this section shall be construed as authorizing individuals or corporations to organize, maintain or employ an armed body of men." By comparison, shortly after the Civil War, Maryland amended its constitutional bill of rights to permit the General Assembly to pass laws "to promote volunteer militia organizations."

When New Mexico became a state in 1912, its constitution expressed a point of view directly opposite that of Illinois. Article 6 of the New Mexico bill of rights reads: "No municipality or county shall regulate, in any way, an incident of the right to keep and bear arms." The state itself has no licensing or permit requirements, although it classifies as "misconduct" the sale, possession or transportation of "prohibited weapons" such as sawed-off rifles and shotguns, automatics and explosives.

Nevada, which entered the Union in 1864 with the standard arms guarantee in its constitution, revised that document in 1982 to ensure that this right would be extended to every citizen "for security and defense, for lawful hunting and recreational use and for other [undefined] purposes."

State penalties for breaches of gun-control laws vary as widely as the controls themselves. They range in severity from Florida's provision that any fatality resulting from the use of a "destructive device" is a capital crime punishable by death, to Idaho's brief section on firearms which, in two short paragraphs, states that anyone who carries a concealed weapon or delivers a weapon to a minor under 16 without the consent of the parent or guardian is guilty of a misdemeanor.

Between these two extremes are infractions that call for a variety of fines or prison terms. Idaho doesn't specify what the penalty will be for supplying a minor with a weapon, but Alabama makes this offense subject to a fine of from $50 to $500. Possession of a machine gun, which most states make illegal, calls for a jail term of up to two years in Pennsylvania, from one to five years in Georgia, Tennessee and Rhode Island and from one to ten years in Louisiana. Maryland makes the use of explosive devices subject to imprisonment for twenty years and/or a fine of $10,000. The same crime in Georgia calls for imprisonment for a term of one to ten years. In Maryland and Massachusetts, possession of a "Molotov cocktail or similar device" earns a sentence of up to five years.

Most often, specific penalties are not cited in weapons legislation. But each unlawful act is classified as one or another grade of felony or misdemeanor, each of which carries its own scale of penalties that are provided in other sections of the state's criminal code. Because conviction of a felony frequently means not only imprisonment but the loss of such privileges as voting and public employment, this category of crime assumes greater importance than a misdemeanor. Even here, states differ in their attitudes toward illegal acts involving weapons. The sale or possession of a silencer is proscribed in most jurisdictions. But Minnesota, Mississippi and

Pennsylvania regard an infraction of that law as only a misdemeanor, while Connecticut, Hawaii, Kansas, Missouri, New York, Rhode Island, South Dakota and Vermont punish it as a felony.

Where the state constitution or law permits local government units to establish their own gun controls, as in Illinois, the results have demonstrated that the impact of the free trade in arms is more readily felt at the municipal level than in Congress. As the record clearly shows, senators and representatives are likely to be influenced less by questions of public welfare and more by their own attitudes toward gun ownership as well as by the money and influence the NRA can bring to bear. Moreover, Washington legislators know that in a national election gun control is rarely if ever a significant campaign issue, that a public stand on this issue will have little effect except to arouse the opposition or support of well-heeled gun organizations. An anti-gun-control speech will bring substantial campaign contributions, while an opposite stand will do little to swell campaign coffers or to influence voters, whose major concerns are jobs, taxes and the cost of living.

The people of Morton Grove, Illinois (population 22,408) saw the threat posed by persons with handguns as immediate and personal. For that reason the town passed an ordinance banning not only the sale of handguns but their possession as well. Evanston, a city of 74,000 and three times the size of Morton Grove, enacted legislation that prohibits the "sale, exchange, rental or other transfer of weapons, firearms, handguns or ammunition," although it stopped short of banning possession of arms purchased prior to enactment of that law.[26] Fifteen other Illinois cities and towns have approved laws governing one or another type of weapon. Chicago requires all handguns to be registered by their owners and will not issue a certificate of ownership to any new purchaser without clearance from the Police Department.

Many cities in other states have also taken action to place restrictions on the sale or ownership of firearms, although in most cases the limits they impose are less severe than those applied in Chicago and Morton Grove. Regulations adopted by cities in Alaska still show the influence of frontier life. That state's most populous community, Anchorage, merely "restricts the age at which it is lawful for a person to purchase or receive a firearm."[27] Fairbanks, whose 30,000 residents live in the heart of the frontier area, simply requires a dealer in that city to be licensed to sell firearms. Over 100 cities and towns in California have passed similar laws on juvenile purchase of firearms and licensing of dealers, but most have additional restrictions regarding the possession of handguns and, in some cases, assault rifles.

Examples of ordinances aimed at control of specific types of weapons can be found in many parts of the country. East Haven, Connecticut, has in common with a number of cities an ordinance restricting the sale of pistols to individuals other than police or military personnel. In Pennsylvania, Philadelphia and Pittsburgh have banned the sale of assault weapons to private individuals. Wilmington, Delaware, prohibits the sale or possession of "armor-piercing ammunition, smooth-bore shot revolver, zip gun, Lazer gun, and coverted tear gas or starter pistol."[28] Some thirty-five cities in Ohio have adopted a variety of gun-control ordinances.

Oldest of the more strict controls are those in New York—city and state—which date back to the Sullivan Law, passed by the state legislature in 1910. But the nation's capital has the most exacting code of laws relating to firearms. Under the heading of "Health and Safety," a chapter on firearms control declares that "in order to promote the health, safety and welfare of the people of the District of Columbia it is necessary to":

1. Require the registration of all firearms that are owned by private citizens;
2. Limit the types of weapons persons may lawfully possess;
3. Assure that only qualified persons are allowed to possess firearms;
4. Regulate deadly weapons dealers; and
5. Make it more difficult for firearms, destructive devices, and ammunition to move in illicit commerce within the District of Columbia.[29]

The small print of regulations aimed at achieving these objectives states that no registration certificate will be approved for a machine gun, sawed-off shotgun, short-barreled rifle or pistol of any kind except to pistol owners whose weapons were validly registered in 1976, prior to enactment of this law. Approved certificates are issued only by the Police Department, and only after the department is satisfied that the prospective gun owner is 21 or older, has not been convicted of a crime or violence or a drug offense, has not in the previous five years been in a mental institution or won acquittal of a crime by reason of insanity, has no record of negligent use of a firearm and no physical disability that would make handling a firearm dangerous. Each applicant for a gun license must submit a recent photograph of himself and, at the police chief's discretion, may be fingerprinted as part of the identification check. The Police Department may take up to 60 days for its background check of the prospective purchaser of a firearm. Procedures for licensing and controlling firearms dealers are spelled out in equally detailed fashion. Limits on the sale of weapons to minors, mental incompetents, felons, alcoholics and drug addicts have been adopted by many jurisdictions, but few require such meticulous investigation and record keeping as the District of Columbia.

Anticontrol forces proved more influential in 1982. Several states added freedom-to-bear-arms provisions to their constitutions, and two municipalities—one in Oregon and one in Georgia—went a step further. Georgia and Oregon are neither the most strict nor the most permissive in their regulation of firearms. Both allow local jurisdictions to legislate on this subject. In 1982 the communities of Kennesaw, Georgia, and Chiloquin, Oregon, approved ordinances *requiring* every household to have a firearm.[30] One Kennesaw council member stated that this action had been taken in response to Morton Grove's outlawing of handguns. A few years later, when the police chief of Kennesaw invited his Morton Grove counterpart to send all confiscated guns to the Kennesaw Police Department, the head of Georgia's Atlanta police took a very different view of the situation. In a letter to members of the National Coalition to Ban Handguns (NCBH), Police Commissioner George Napper expressed his anger at "those slick full-color 'I'm the NRA' magazine ads," particularly one which illustrated a police officer "extolling the strong bond between the National Rifle Association and the police." Charging the NRA with defending the sale and possession of handguns, machine guns and "copkiller bullets," Napper said he was "outraged by the NRA's steadfast, reckless disregard for the safety of law enforcement officers." Two years later, Commissioner Napper wrote an even longer letter urging NCBH members to support nationwide handgun and assault-weapon laws and denouncing the NRA for trying to "manipulate the black community into believing" that Maryland's Saturday-night-special ban "was bad for them."[31]

From this brief canvass of state and municipal legislation it is clear that very few communities in the United States accept the notion that government has no right to interfere in any way with the right of its citizens to possess whatever weapons they choose, either for recreation or for protection of home and country. Nevertheless, the traffic in guns for self-protection has been spurred by the increasing number of violent crimes. But these same circumstances have sharpened public awareness of the need to curtail the availability of weapons that may bring death or disability to so many, whether by accident or design.

Gun enthusiasts contest the right of Congress to ban private possession of almost any weapon, including the machine gun that the majority of states have declared to be too dangerous to be left in private hands. In this respect, many state legislatures have come a long way from the early days of completely free trade in firearms. And in exercising their police power to protect citizens against the dangers inherent in unrestricted proliferation of lethal weapons, they have been sustained by the courts, almost without exception.

5

What the Courts Have Said

A full century after the Declaration of Independence, the only states that had been formed out of the immense area from the Dakotas and Oklahoma westward to the Pacific Ocean were California, Oregon and Nevada. Colorado was admitted to the Union in 1876, but it was not until 1889–1890 that North Dakota, South Dakota, Montana, Washington, Idaho and Wyoming completed the northern tier of states, with Oklahoma, Arizona and New Mexico rounding out the southern tier some twenty years later.

For as long as this enormous expanse of territory offered opportunities for pioneering families to expand their horizons, the possession of weapons for hunting and personal protection in that part of the country was taken for granted. In more settled areas, however, the right of a state to exercise control over the possession and, more particularly, the use of weapons, was widely recognized. The first occasion in which this question reached a federal court came in 1876.

In the aftermath of the Civil War, Congress had passed a law, known as the Force Act, making it a crime for two or more persons to conspire to injure or intimidate any citizen with the intent of hindering the free exercise of his legal or constitutional rights. One of the many breaches of that law occurred in Louisiana, where in 1873 an armed white mob stormed a courthouse that several hundred blacks were using for a meeting place. In what came to be known as the Colfax Massacre, the mob set fire to the building and murdered about 100 of its occupants. William Cruikshank and two other leaders of the attack were arrested, charged and convicted of conspiracy under the Force Act. They were set free by a unanimous decision of the U.S. Supreme Court, whose opinion today would read like something out of *Alice in Wonderland*. However, it was delivered at a time when, despite the intentions of the framers of the Fourteenth Amendment, the courts continued to hold that the protections offered by the Constitution's Bill of Rights applied only to the federal government and not to the states. From that perspective, Chief Justice Morrison R. Waite wrote the Court's decision, which, in its essentials, came down to this:

- The right of the people peaceably to assemble for lawful purposes existed long before the adoption of the Constitution of the United States.
- It was not, therefore, a right granted to the people by the Constitution.
- The First Amendment to the Constitution prohibits Congress from abridging the right of the people to assemble and to petition the government for a redress on grievances.
- This, like the other amendments proposed and adopted at the same time, was intended to apply to the national government alone, and was not meant to limit the powers of the state governments with respect to their own citizens.
- For their protection under the First Amendment, therefore, the people must look to the states.[1]

Had Chief Justice Waite and his colleagues on the Supreme Court given the same consideration to the intentions of the men who designed the Fourteenth Amendment as they did the drafters of the federal Bill of Rights, they might have come to a different conclusion. For the originator of the clause that declares that "no State shall . . . deprive any person of life, liberty or property, without due process of law; nor deny to any person within its jurisdiction the equal protection of the laws" made his purpose crystal clear on the floor of the House of Representatives. That purpose, Ohio's John A. Bingham said, was "to arm the Congress of the United States with the power to enforce the Bill of Rights as it stands in the Constitution today." This view was echoed in the Senate by Jacob M. Howard of Michigan, who insisted that the Fourteenth Amendment was needed to force the states to adhere to the federal Bill of Rights and would "forever disable every one of them [the states] from passing laws trenching upon those rights and privileges."[2] In the ensuing, sometimes bitter debate over whether the amendment would give former slaves the right to vote, its specific purpose as defined by Representative Bingham and Senator Howard was never challenged, either in the House or the Senate.

Ignoring the Fourteenth Amendment's legislative history, the Court's logic led to the declaration that Cruikshank was beyond the reach of federal law regarding the use of weapons. The right to bear arms for a lawful purpose, Chief Justice Waite said, "is not a right granted by the Constitution." Nor, he added, is it dependent on the Constitution for its existence. "The Second Amendment declares that it shall not be infringed; but this, as has been seen, means no more than that it shall not be infringed by Congress." Hence, protection against civil rights violations by one citizen against another must be provided by "municipal legislation" and the local police.[3]

Blatantly unjust as this attitude was to tens of thousands of black citizens, who could expect no protection from state governments that within a decade after the Civil War had reverted to control by white segregationists, the Court's decision nevertheless made clear that the states were free to adopt any laws regarding the possession and use of weapons they thought necessary.

One of the control measures taken by the state of Illinois was to require "any body of men" other than the state militia to obtain a license if they wished to "associate themselves together as a military company or organize or to drill on parade with arms."[4] When Herman Presser, leader of a privately organized company, was charged with violating that law, he challenged it as a breach of his rights under the Second and Fourteenth Amendments of the Constitution. Every citizen, he argued, "has secured to him the right to keep and bear arms as part of the militia which Congress has the right to organize and to arm and drill companies." When Congress had, under Article 1, Section 8, of the Constitution, provided for a "uniform militia throughout the United States," Presser said its intent was that "absolutely all able bodied citizens of the state be enrolled in the militia." No state, he contended, may legislate on the same subject or leave it to the governor to decide how and when to organize the militia. Therefore, the Illinois statute under which he was indicted was an invasion of his rights as a U.S. citizen.[5]

Every aspect of Presser's argument was rejected by the Supreme Court in 1886. Citing the earlier Cruikshank case, Justice William B. Woods denied that the state was precluded from enacting laws to govern the organization of the militia, or that such laws infringed on the right of the people to bear arms. The state, he declared, had not only the right, but "the bounden duty" to provide for the safety of its people by any means that are not constrained by the Constitution or laws of the United States. "We have not been referred to any statute of the United States," Justice Woods said, "which confers upon the plaintiff the privilege which he asserts." Further, the justice pointed out that "the right voluntarily to associate together as a military company . . . independent of an act of Congress or law of the state authorizing the same, is not an attribute of national citizenship." On the contrary, he said, "Military organization and military drill and parade under arms are subjects especially under the control of the government in every country."[6]

Eight years later, a Texan who had been convicted of murder appealed his death sentence and challenged the state law against carrying dangerous weapons in public as an infringement of the Second Amendment right of the people to keep and bear arms. He further charged that under the Fourth Amendment he had been illegally subjected to search and seizure. Sustaining the position of the Texas court, the U.S. Supreme Court found no evidence that the defendant had been denied any constitutional rights. And, in the tradition of the times, the Court added that "even if he were [denied such rights], it is well settled that the restrictions of these amendments operate only upon the Federal power, and have no reference whatever to proceedings in state courts."[7]

The twentieth century brought a marked change in attitude toward the federal government's responsibility for the protection of civil rights. This was evident not only in Supreme Court decisions, but in public pressure for laws that would guarantee such protection and in congressional debates on the subject. A new slant in the legal approach came with the gradual acceptance by the courts of the position set forth in 1866 by the two primary sponsors of the Fourteenth Amendment, Representative John A. Bingham and Senator Jacob M. Howard.

Considering the Supreme Court's nineteenth-century economic philosphy, it is not surprising that its first acknowledgment that the federal Bill of Rights might affect state action came in a case involving property rights rather than civil liberties. Just three years before the end of the century, the Court decided that the due process clause of the Fourteenth Amendment assured Fifth Amendment protection against any state attempting to take private property without compensation.[8]

Another twenty-eight years passed before the Court saw fit to apply the same logic to First Amendment freedoms. It did this in a case involving a New York State law that made advocacy of revolution as a means of overthrowing the government a crime. Although the Court upheld that law, it acknowledged that "freedom of speech and of the press . . . are among the fundamental personal rights and 'liberties' protected by the due process clause of the Fourteenth Amendment from impairment by the states."[9]

No new appeal to Second Amendment rights was made until 1939. At that point, two Arkansas residents "did unlawfully, knowingly, wilfully and feloniously, transport in interstate commerce . . . a double barrel 12-gauge Stevens shotgun having a barrel less than 18 inches in length." Prosecuted and found guilty of breaking the National Firearms Act of 1934, which included a ban on interstate commerce in sawed-off shotguns, the defendants protested that this was a usurpation of police power reserved to the states and was a breach of their rights under the Second Amendment. A federal district court agreed that the National Firearms Act violated the Second Amendment, but the Supreme Court refused to accept that argument. Stressing the tie between the right to bear arms and the need for an organized militia, the Court traced this association back to the days of King Alfred, who ruled England from 871 to 899 A.D. Reversing the lower court's decision, Justice James C. McReynolds concluded the high court's opinion in this fashion:

In the absence of any evidence tending to show that possession or use of a "shotgun having a barrel of less than eighteen inches in length" at this time has some reasonable relationship to the preservation or efficiency of a well regulated militia, we cannot say that the Second Amendment guarantees the right to keep and bear such an instrument.[10]

More than 40 years after this decision was handed down, an organization calling itself the Second Amendment Foundation joined the National Rifle Association in attacking all forms of gun control. Responding to rising public anger at the number of deaths caused by people using cheap handguns—so-called Saturday night specials—the foundation's executive director attempted to use the Supreme Court's position in the 1939 case to support his organization's view of the right to bear arms. In a letter published in the *New York Times*, Donald A. Feder referred to the passage quoted above—not quite accurately, but closely enough—to make the point that the Court was concerned only with the right to "possess and carry a sawed-off shotgun." He went on to state, quite inaccurately, that "by implication" the Court had supported the gun owners' long-standing belief that all citizens are "members of the unorganized militia."[11]

The fact is that after reviewing only the early history of the need for an organized militia at a time when standing armies were regarded as a threat to liberty, the Court implied nothing whatever about the current status of the militia. Rather, it devoted only a single paragraph to an observation that "most if not all states have adopted provisions touching the right to keep and bear arms," noting that differences in statutory language have "led to somewhat variant conclusions concerning the scope of the right guaranteed." The word "militia" never appeared in this brief reference to modern practice.[12]

As to Feder's reference to what he called "The Militia Act of 1792," his quotation included only a single phrase from one of several laws passed that year, citing a provision that said "every free able-bodied white male" citizen from 18 to 45 years of age was to be enrolled in the militia. Feder omitted several important facts about the 1792 legislation. His quotation was accurate as far as it went, but it stopped short of revealing that the so-called "definition" of militia included the statement that identified enrollers as "citizens of the respective states," not all free white males, and not in their capacity as citizens of the United States. Further, they were to be enrolled "by a captain or commanding officer of the company within whose bounds such citizens shall reside." The significance of this last provision lies in the fact that the militia was to be organized "as the legislature of each state shall direct," and was to be "officered by the respective states" in a manner that would match the arrangement used by the regular army. That is, federal rules regarding the number of officers of each rank would apply, but each state would select and appoint the officers, who would receive their orders "from the commander-in-chief of the state."[13] Moreover, a law passed prior to the one cited by Feder made it clear that when the president of the United States calls upon the militia to repel an invasion or suppress an insurrection, he would take command of contingents normally under state control.[14]

When Feder concluded with a statement that to this day federal law includes "a variant" of the 1792 definition of militia, he was referring to a section of the *U.S. Code* that reads, in full, as follows:

The militia of the United States consists of all able-bodied males at least 17 years of age and, except as provided in section 313 of title 32, under 45 years of age who are, or who have made a declaration of intention to become citizens of the United States, and of female citizens of the United States who are commissioned officers of the National Guard.
The classes of the militia are—

(1) the organized militia, which consists of the National Guard and the Naval Militia; and

(2) the unorganized militia, which consists of the members of the militia who are not members of the National Guard or the Naval Militia.[15]

Except for a list of exemptions, principally federal employees, mariners and those on active duty in the armed forces, there is no further refinement of this definition. The National Guard and Naval Militia are distinct units supported by appropriations made annually by Congress. The unorganized militia refers to those state citizens who, *under state law*, are subject to call in an emergency declared by the governor. In enacting this legislation, Congress has shown no intent to alter the traditional concept of the militia as a military force that is to be organized and controlled by the states under federal guidelines only as to types of units, kinds of training, arms and equipment, and officer–enlisted man ratios.

Few of the more recent challenges to federal, state and local gun controls have been carried as far as the U.S. Supreme Court. A broad defense of the National Firearms Act was upheld by a federal circuit court of appeals in 1942, in a decision that stated:

The right to keep and bear arms is not a right conferred upon the people by the federal Constitution. Whatever rights in this respect the people may have depend upon local legislation; the only function of the Second Amendment being to prevent the federal government, and the federal government only, from infringing that right.[16]

This principle was reinforced some thirty years later when another appellate court upheld a conviction for violation of the Omnibus

Crime Control and Safe Streets Act of 1968 for illegal possession of a firearm, saying: "Since the Second Amendment right 'to keep and bear arms' applies only to the right of the state to maintain a militia and not to the individual's right to bear arms, there can be no serious claim to any express constitutional right of an individual to possess a firearm."[17]

"Mere possession" of a weapon had previously been held to be a punishable offense under the National Firearm Act, and a challenge to the constitutionality of that part of the law had been turned away by the Supreme Court in 1961.[18]

A critical test of local gun control legislation came in a 1981 confrontation between the general public and National Rifle Association members and supporters when the voters in a small Illinois town approved an ordinance banning possession of many of the weapons in common use by criminals, from blackjacks to assault weapons, including "any handgun, unless the same has been rendered permanently inoperative." Exempt from the law were peace officers, military personnel and others who could show a legitimate need for a particular weapon. Although the law made clear that it was not to be applied to hunting rifles and shotguns, target pistols and antique weapons, or to licensed gun clubs, collectors and dealers, the NRA mounted a nationwide campaign to have this popular verdict overturned.[19]

Taken initially to an Illinois state court, attorneys for the village of Morton Grove had the case moved to a federal district court. Plaintiff's attorneys concentrated their attack on the ban on handguns, asserting that this provision violated Article I, Section 22, of the Illinois constitution and the Second, Ninth and Fourteenth Amendments of the U.S. Constitution. The verdict of district court Judge Bernard Decker was that under the state constitution "the right to keep and bear arms in Illinois was so limited by police power" that the Morton Grove ban on handguns violated no rights under either the state or the U.S. Constitution.[20]

On appeal, plaintiffs received a sympathetic hearing from one of the three judges in the circuit court. Judge Coffey believed the Morton Grove ordinance to be "an impermissible attempt to address an issue which the people of the State of Illinois through their elected representatives have deemed to be a matter properly resolved by state action." In addition, Judge Coffey reverted to the doctrine of original intent, saying, "As a matter of constitutional law," the ordinance permitted "an intrusion on our basic rights as citizens which would no doubt be alarming and odious to our founding fathers."[21]

Judges Bauer and Wood viewed the matter in a different light, holding that the appellate court was bound by the Supreme Court's decision in the Presser case. Citing plaintiff's agreement that "Presser is controlling," the court offered this judgment of plaintiff's interpretation of that earlier decision:

It is difficult to understand how appellants can assert that Presser supports the theory that the second amendment right to keep and bear arms is a fundamental right which the state cannot regulate when the Presser decision plainly states that "[t]he Second Amendment declares that it shall not be infringed, but this . . . has no other effect than to restrict the powers of the National government. . . ." This argument borders on the frivolous and does not warrant any further consideration.[22]

The position taken by the circuit court did not satisfy the plaintiff, who requested a further review by the U.S. Supreme Court. But here he was rebuffed again, the high court refusing to hear to case.[23]

One further contest arose over an ordinance passed by the Chicago City Council that required that all firearms within that jurisdiction be registered with the city. This part of the municipal code also classified some firearms, including handguns, as "unregisterable," or illegal, if procured or brought into the city after passage of the law. Again, the complaint was that the ordinance deprived Jerome Sklar of his rights under the federal Constitution as well as the Illinois state constitution. And again, citing the decision in Quilici v. Morton Grove, both district and circuit courts rejected that contention.[24]

A legal quarrel of a different sort was instigated by a federal statute that required membership in the National Rifle Association to be able to buy U.S. Army rifles at a discount.[25] Unlike the cases discussed earlier, this was a civil action in which the constitutionality of the law was challenged because it "directs the Department of the Army to sell firearms at cost to members of the National Rifle Association of America" as part of a Civilian Marksmanship program.[26] The law had been on the books since 1903, and had been designed "for the purpose of improving marksmanship skills among citizens in order that those called to military service might be more proficient marksmen and require less training." However, the exclusive privilege of buying guns by NRA members only was written into the law in 1924.[27]

The court's review of the history of the program revealed that after World War II, when sales figures became available, "during the period 1960 to 1967 the Army sold tens of thousands of firearms each year to NRA members," sales including rifles, shotguns, and pistols. The record also indicated that the administration of President Jimmy Carter suggested the program be discontinued because of the "introduction of sophisticated weaponry and revisions of wartime tactics." When this was formally proposed in the U.S. Senate, it was defeated by a wide margin.[28] In the House, members of the Investigations Subcommittee of the Armed Services Committee showed their support for the NRA by recommending "that some several hundred thousand surplus rifles scheduled for destruction be sold instead in unlimited quantities under the auspices of the Civilian Marksmanship Program."[29]

In 1979, Geoffrey S. Gavett applied for purchase of a rifle from the army. His application was rejected because he was not a member of the National Rifle Association. With the support of the National Coalition to Ban Handguns (NCBH), Gavett sued to have the law declared unconstitutional on the ground that it denied him equal protection of the law by preventing him from purchasing a rifle at a discount from the army "while granting such a right to members of the National Rifle Association who in every other respect have the same qualifications and are in every other way similarly situated."[30]

Interestingly enough, although the army supported the NRA in defense of the discriminatory character of the law, the Department of Justice advised the court that the executive branch would not defend the law against plaintiff's claim of unconstitutionality. The department's view was that "this requirement [of NRA membership for the purchase of army guns] does not bear a rational relationship to any legitimate governmental interest and is therefore unconstitutional."[31] In the light of this opinion, the court deferred consideration of the case for 45 days to allow Congress to file its own defense of the statute. But Congress never responded to this invitation.

In reaching a decision, the court said, "The NRA argument, most broadly, comes down to this: the training of civilian Americans in marksmanship is a program vital to this country's defense, and only the NRA can, as a practical matter, provide such training."

Pointing out that "there are obvious alternative means of training citizens of military age in marksmanship skills," the court asserted that even if that were not true, it would not be in the interest of the government "to perpetuate a monopoly on an important aspect of national defense with a private organization . . . particularly when that group is at the same time significantly engaged in lobbying the government and otherwise attempting to influence it on controversial public issues." The same logic would apply, Judge Harold Greene said, whether the private organization was the NRA, the NCBH, the ACLU, the AFL-CIO, the American Legion, or the U.S. Chamber of Commerce.[32]

What the court refused to do was to declare the entire statute unconstitutional. It accepted as valid the general purpose of the law, which was to provide the country with marksmen in the event of war. However, it found that the section of the law "which requires membership in the National Rifle Association as a precondition to the purchase of Army surplus rifles unconstitutionally deprives plaintiff of the equal protection of the Fifth Amendment to the Constitution."[33]

At this writing, other gun-control problems pending before the U.S. Supreme Court include the question of whether Congress may ban the possession of guns near school buildings and whether local police can be required to enforce the Brady law. The latter case arises out of a suit by five rural sheriffs in Texas, Louisiana and Mississippi. Financed by the National Rifle Association, four of the sheriffs argue that by making local police responsible for overseeing the 5-day waiting period and making background checks on purchasers of handguns, Congress has intruded into an area "reserved to the States" by the Tenth Amendment. They also challenge the Brady law as a violation of the Second Amendment guarantee of the "right of the people to keep and bear arms."[34]

Notwithstanding the many court decisions that have made clear that the Second Amendment does not guarantee every individual the right to possess and bear arms and that such a right is protected at the state and local level only to the extent that it contributes to the objective of maintaining an organized militia under the direction of state-appointed officers, the NRA continues to disseminate information and opinions contrary to these court-determined facts. Almost every public statement by an NRA official and every issue of the two monthly journals published by that organization warn of the threat to "those rights guaranteed under the Second Amendment." What is called a threat invariably turns out to be any proposal to limit or control the private purchase of any kind of weapon—from pistols or assault rifles to field artillery—as the NRA insists that the Second Amendment must be interpreted to "encompass all 'arms,'" not just weapons used for sport.[35] As the next chapter will indicate, this does not accord with the general public's view of gun control.

6

What the Public Thinks

No greater change in public attitudes toward the possession and use of guns can be imagined than that which evolved from the days of our revolutionary forebears to more recent years. Early Americans were, almost without exception, of one mind on the subject of gun ownership. Private possession of rifles, shotguns and pistols was considered essential for putting meat on the table and for protecting both the family and the community from attack, whether by thugs, hostile Indian tribes or foreign invaders. As earlier chapters have indicated, that view changed little, if at all, well into the twentieth century.

Prior to the Civil War, state laws prohibiting the sale of guns to slaves were common enough, especially after a slave revolt led by Nat Turner resulted in the death of fifty-eight members of slave-holding families. But laws to protect slave owners against uprisings were thought of in much the same way as laws making it a crime to take up arms against the government. Statutes of the latter variety became more common as post–Civil War conflicts between haves and have-nots increased with industrialization, and so-called alien ideologies were seen as a threat to established relations between various elements of society. However, the legislation produced by these threats to traditional living came largely in the form of criminal syndicalism statutes. Even the assassinations of Presidents Lincoln, Garfield and McKinley by pistol-wielding malcontents did not elicit demands for legislation to curb the sale of handguns to private individuals.

Prohibition and the gang wars for control of the illegal manufacture and sale of liquor put the subject of guns in a new light in the 1920s. But the initial reaction to gangsterism was not to curtail private ownership of guns but to arm the previously unarmed members of the agency responsible for enforcing federal prohibition laws: the Federal Bureau of Investigation. Any awareness among the general public of a need to curtail private possession of guns was not discernible until it was revealed by the newly emerging public opinion polls. The pattern of opinion on this subject can be traced through an examination of the Gallup polls, which have been compiled and published in book form for every year since 1935.

The first time the Gallup organization felt the gun problem worthy of inquiry was in the spring of 1938. The question asked then was whether handgun owners should be required to register their weapons "with the Government." An overwhelming majority of 84 percent said Yes.[1]

World War II and the subsequent cold war turned the country's attention to other problems. But the internal strife generated in the late 1950s and 1960s by the Vietnam War, the assassination of President Kennedy, the murder of civil rights workers in Mississippi and riots that wreaked death and destruction in Los Angeles, Detroit and Newark brought the subject of guns into sharp focus.

In 1959 Gallup returned to the problem of gun control. A simple question asked people if they would favor or oppose a requirement that a police permit be obtained before an individual could purchase a gun. As in 1938, a substantial 75 percent of those polled favored such a law. Even more significant was the response of those who already owned guns or who used guns for hunting. Some 65 percent of gun owners and 62 percent of the hunters supported a licensing requirement.[2]

A more in-depth inquiry posed the same question four years later, with responses broken down by age, sex, education and geographical region. Overall, 78 percent favored a permit requirement, a figure that increased to 85 percent where women were concerned. A similar response came from 81 percent of those with a high school education, 80 percent from college graduates and 74 percent from people with only a grade school education. In the three age groups—21–29, 30–49, 50 and over—the youngest set showed the lowest rate of approval, but this was still almost three-quarters (74 percent) of the group. In the middle group, 81 percent approved, as did 78 percent of those 50 and over. Regionally, the highest approval rate of 90 percent came in the East, the lowest—72 percent—in the South, with people in the Midwest and Far West showing 77 percent and 73.5 percent approval, respectively.[3]

In 1967, following race riots in Newark and Detroit, the question of a police permit was raised again, and this time the results were broken down by race. Interestingly enough, only three percentage points separated the approval rates of whites and blacks, both favoring a permit law by majorities of 73 percent of whites and 70 percent of blacks.[4]

Although private possession of guns has for most of this century been associated with crime, that connection was treated differently in the sixties than it was later. During the earlier period questions put to a sample of the general population usually dealt with the causes of crime or the adequacy of penalties given convicted criminals. When asked in 1964 to assign responsibility for the increase in crime, 41 percent named parents, and only 18 percent pointed to lax law enforcement. But four years later, when the question focused specifically on the adequacy of penalties applied to criminals, a substantial majority thought the courts had not been harsh enough in their sentences. The group that was critical of the courts rose from 63 percent in 1968 to 75 percent only a year later.[5] And although opinion on that particular point has not been regularly tested in more recent years, the theme of insufficient punishment has been a major part of the NRA campaign to discredit gun control proposals. "Guns don't kill people, people kill people" is a slogan the NRA has attempted to drill into the public consciousness.

In 1969 crime and guns were tied together in a question regarding the advisability of doubling the regular sentence for anyone who commits a crime with a gun. Some 58 percent thought that a good idea, 33 percent regarded it as bad, and a larger than usual 9 percent had no opinion.[6]

Drugs replaced guns as the subject of criminal action in 1970. Three years earlier only 2 percent of people polled on the causes of crime thought addiction to drugs or alcohol was a major factor. By 1970 drugs had assumed such importance that when asked what penalties should be applied to users or pushers, a majority of respondents urged substantial prison terms. Users were thought by

27 percent to deserve 2 to 5 years, by 23 percent 10 years or more. For pushers, 10 percent would sentence them to 2 to 5 years, 43 percent would give 10 years or more, 24 percent thought a life term appropriate, and 4 percent voted for the death penalty.[7]

Concern over gun control paralleled the rising fear of drug use. In 1972 a nationwide canvass of opinion on the desirability of requiring a police permit to purchase a gun produced a 71 percent favorable response. And again, a majority of 61 percent of gun owners said they approved such a requirement.[8] The question was important enough in that presidential year to be included in a further poll of opinion on matters that would influence a voter's attitude toward candidates for the presidency. When asked whether they would be more or less likely to vote for someone who advocated stricter control of firearms, 62 percent replied that this would make them more likely to support such a candidate.[9] Two years later gun control was one of fourteen issues facing contestants for congressional seats. Questioned about these issues, 72 percent of the voters said they would support a requirement that all firearms be registered.[10]

Politically, the problem was put into better perspective in the next (1976) presidential election, when respondents were asked to rate the importance of each of twenty issues. On that occasion, popular concern over inflation, the high cost of living, government spending, unemployment, crime, tax reform, the energy situation, lack of trust in government, welfare, national health care and defense spending all were rated more important than gun control.[11] So despite the fact that 46 percent gave gun control their top rating or next to the top, this was clearly an issue that would not turn the election. Knowing this, procontrol candidates could gain little if anything from beating this drum, while anticontrol advocates could at least be assured of contributions from gun clubs and promoters of the Second Amendment argument.

Throughout the 1970s and 1980s, when the subject was treated independently of political campaigns, public opinion continued to be strongly in favor of stricter controls over the sale and ownership of guns. Regardless of whether the question was put in terms of licensing to purchase a gun, licensing to carry a gun outside the home, stricter control of handguns in particular or a waiting period to permit a background check of the prospective purchaser, a substantial majority of the public invariably indicated a desire for tighter controls. And despite the vast increase in progun propaganda by the NRA and other organizations of similar mind, there has since been no weakening in the nationwide support for greater restrictions on gun sales and ownership. Only when the proposal was to ban completely the possession of handguns to anyone but police and others given special authorization did the approval rate fall to less than one-third. But in the same poll that posed the question in that manner, 59 percent said they thought laws governing the sale of handguns should be more strict, and 75 percent indicated their approval of a law requiring a license to carry a gun outside the home. The latter group included 65 percent of gun owners.[12] Clearly, by this time the general public had come to accept Supreme Court Justice O'Connor's admonition that in deciding on a marked change in policy, it is necessary to consider "whether facts have so changed or come to be seen so differently, as to have robbed the old rule of significant application or justification."[13]

Even as these 1979 figures were being published, Gallup reported that gun ownership was widespread in the United States. A note accompanying the poll cited above included the following observations:

While there is a great deal of controversy surrounding the entire subject of gun control and what steps, if any, should be taken to combat gun-related accidents and crimes, there is one aspect of the problem that is beyond dispute—there are plenty of guns in the hands of Americans. Almost every other home (49%) has at least one gun, with the incidence of ownership reaching 53% in the South and 70% in the smaller communities and rural areas.

Rifles and shotguns are more popular with the public than are pistols and revolvers, with three households in ten having either a shotgun or rifle. About two in every ten have a pistol or revolver.[14]

The proliferation of guns in private hands, which paralleled the increasing incidence of violence nationwide, did not go unnoticed elsewhere. A 1986 poll conducted in England revealed that 62 percent of the British people believed the level of violent crime in the United States made it an unsafe country to live in.[15] This occurred at a time when Great Britain was having its own troubles with gang and racial conflicts. But as a later chapter makes clear, neither British experience nor the problems of other countries can match the devastating effect that the absence of adequate gun controls has had in the United States. If we simply compare the

Table 6.1
Deaths from Wartime Battle and Peacetime Gunfire

	No. of Deaths	Period of Time*	Daily Average	Annual Average
World War I	53,513	4/6/17-11/11/18	93.4	34,085
World War II	292,131	12/7/41-8/15/45	217.0	79,383
Korean War	33,651	6/27/50-7/27/53	29.9	10,926
Vietnam War	47,369	8/2/64-8/11/72	16.2	5,906
Persian Gulf	148	1/17/91-3/3/91	3.2	- -
Peacetime 1990	36,866	1/1/90-12/31/90	101.0	36,866

Sources: *World Almanac* 1992, FBI *Uniform Crime Reports* for 1990.

*From declaration of war or first military action to armistice or removal of troops.

death rate from gun-related violence in our "peacetime" society with deaths from what has always been considered the ultimate form of violence—war—a rather startling picture appears (see Table 6.1). Only during the most devastating war of the twentieth century was the rate of killing higher than among the general population during the peacetime year of 1990.

In the 1988 election year, the drug problem emerged as the public's most pressing concern. Despite a federal "Just say no" campaign led by President and Mrs. Reagan, and increasing efforts to cut into the traffic in cocaine, heroin and marijuana, both at the U.S. borders and by cooperation with the governments of Colombia and Mexico, drug use seemed as widespread as ever. Voter opinion on the eleven policy issues most frequently discussed during the presidential campaign showed a higher percentage of the electorate concerned with "reducing drug supply" than with any other problem. Among Bush voters even "strengthening defense" fell ten points short of the 82 percent who worried about drugs. Of Dukakis supporters, only 37 percent believed strengthening defense was as important as reducing drugs, the latter given top priority by 86 percent of those polled.[16]

As the 1980s came to a close, repeated incidents of mass killings focused public concern on the danger posed by private possession of automatic and semiautomatic weapons—commonly referred to as assault weapons. Members of Congress who believed there is no valid reason for any private person to own a weapon of that sort, and who were not intimidated by the NRA, submitted or supported bills to tighten federal controls over such weapons. Newspapers and magazines entered the battle editorially, most of them standing squarely behind stricter controls. *Field and Stream*, a magazine dedicated to the enjoyment of hunting and fishing, asked its readers to respond to the question "Should shooters be entitled to buy any type of firearm, or should rapid-firing guns of military origin be sold only to collectors under Treasury Department license?" Of the 681 replies, 81 percent said yes, "shooters *should* be able to buy any type of gun" (magazine's emphasis).[17] The comments offered by this group echoed the statements of NRA officials in that organization's official journal:

In my opinion, it is our elected representatives who need to be brought under control.

Instead of locking up the guns, let's try a novel approach: let's lock up the guy who breaks the law with the gun.

We do not have a firearms problem. Our problem is the near-absence of an effective criminal justice system.

It is amazing that even a magazine with hunters' interests foremost can make the same idiotic mistakes about semi-automatic rifles that the gungrabbing media make.[18]

Despite the overwhelming opposition to gun controls shown by the correspondence of most readers who felt strongly enough to respond to the survey, the dissenting votes, along with examples of misplaced law enforcement, led the magazine to head its article, "Survey Results and a Tale of Confusion." The confusion was attributed to those well-meaning persons—including lawmakers—who don't realize how the regulations or laws they propose would harm honest citizens, and who would reverse their judgments if they were enlightened on this subject by gun owners who could explain the "realities" of the situation.

The realities seemed apparent enough to the minority of *Field and Stream* readers who voted against unlimited gun purchases. One wrote, "There is no tradition of civilians owning assault-type guns," adding, "Any hunter who has to use more than two rounds to bag his game doesn't deserve to be called a hunter." Another, who said he had been a hunter since the age of seven, concluded that "after much thought, I can see no justification for me—or others like me—to own a paramilitary assault rifle." His advice was, "Reserve that kind of firepower for the police and the military." A Vietnam veteran, who scarcely had to explain that he was "familiar with assault rifles," said that "for practical reasons, I would never own one even for home defense. If a person wants to buy such a weapon, let them ... but have the magazine plugged so that it holds no more than five rounds." And a former NRA member who reported being "fed up with the NRA position" reminded readers that "assault rifles are to the sport of hunting as pornography is to literature."[19]

The heat generated by this controversy was felt as strongly in Washington as anywhere else. In increasing numbers, members of the Senate and House of Representatives felt called upon to intro- duce bills dealing with private possession of handguns, assault weapons and the deadlier types of ammunition. The year 1989 saw eight such bills submitted for consideration of the Senate, while nineteen were offered in the House. Except for those that were limited to mandating jail terms for crimes committed with a gun, every other bill became a target for the NRA to shoot at. The organization's biggest guns were aimed at proposals designed or supported by the more powerful members of legislature. Operating through its Institute for Legislative Action, this combination fund- raising and lobbying organization sought to line up both national and state legislators against any and all laws that would curb in the slightest fashion the manufacture, sale, import, export or private ownership of any kind of weapon or ammunition. Every bill of this kind was carefully monitored, and NRA members were kept ap- prised of the threat by articles in the *American Rifleman* and *American Hunter*. Members were also urged to write or telephone their rep- resentative law makers—at every level of government—to call for their aid in defeating all control measures. Through 1989 these efforts were largely successful, although by that time the growing fear of indiscriminate killing had led to adoption of local gun- control ordinances in many towns and cities across the nation.

The rising tide of public protest over mass murders and the killing of innocent civilians caught in the crossfire of drug and gang wars was expressed in every quarter of the country. All through 1990 and 1991 members of Congress were stimulated to devise new bills on gun control. Best known was the so-called Brady bill, named for its sponsorship by James Brady, former

President Reagan's press secretary who was shot and permanently disabled during the 1981 assassination attempt by John Hinckley. The Brady bill had as its principal objective a 7-day waiting period for the purchase of a handgun. It required the dealer to give the police the name, address and birth date of the prospective buyer, which would allow the police time to check the buyer's background for any record of criminal activity or mental health problems. After 7 days, if the police found no reason to block the sale, the purchase could be completed.

An alternative measure proposed by Representative Harley O. Staggers, Jr. would also have required a background check on handgun purchasers, but not until a nationwide computer network had been established to permit the quickest possible inquiry and response. The contest between backers of these two bills was the center of attention within Congress from 1991 to 1993. Ultimately the Brady bill was passed with modifications that provide for a waiting period of five "business days" that will remain in effect until the computer network recommended by Staggers comes into being, at which point the wait will be reduced to three business days.[20]

Throughout the congressional debate over a waiting period the public persisted in its view that laws governing firearms should be more strict than those passed in 1968. On the specific question of a 7-day waiting period to permit identification of purchasers who are convicted felons or are mentally ill, a March 1991 poll revealed that 93 percent favored such a law. Even the no-opinion vote, characteristically 5 to 10 percent on almost any issue, was less than 1 percent in response to this question. This occurred at a time when 46 percent of those questioned acknowledged having a gun of some kind in the house.[21] Later in the year, as candidates for president began to talk about the upcoming 1992 election, pollees were asked to identify from a list of issues those they would consider important in deciding which candidate to support. Some 79 percent said the candidate's views on gun control should be considered. Of the ten problems offered for comment, only those dealing with national health policy, taxes and job discrimination against women and minorities were ranked higher in importance. Lower on the scale than gun control were abortion, trade with Japan, liberal or conservative leaning, the death penalty, support for the war with Iraq and public assistance to private school parents.[22]

Renewed debate over the Brady bill kept that subject before the public all through 1993. But passage of the bill into law did nothing to calm the growing fear of violence. On the contrary, that fear was reflected in a marked increase in the sale of guns for personal protection. Ironically, an October public opinion poll showed that 89 percent of those questioned considered the availability of guns to be an important (45 percent said critical) factor among the causes of crime.[23] And although a substantial majority continued to believe that controls on the sale of firearms should be made more strict, by year's end the same poll that recorded 64 percent in favor of tighter gun laws also showed 60 percent opposing a law that would make possession of a handgun illegal.[24] The same desire for self-protection appeared in a January 1994 poll, which found only 46 percent favoring a law banning the sale of handguns to anyone except law enforcement officers. That poll also demonstrated that 73 percent believed crime had increased over the previous year, to the point where crime rivaled economic and health problems as an issue of national importance.[25]

7

The Practice in Other Countries

In 1968, when demands for stricter gun controls were spurred by the assassinations of Martin Luther King, Jr., and Senator Robert Kennedy, the *Washington Post* published a survey of conditions in other parts of the world as reported by its foreign correspondents. The results were fairly summarized in the headline, "Gun Curbs Are Stricter in Many Nations than in the U.S."[1] Twenty-two years later a letter circulated to the Washington embassies of sixty-seven countries with which the United States had diplomatic relations requested from them or from their appropriate government agencies two kinds of information: the laws governing private possession of firearms, and statistics on crimes committed with firearms. The responses indicated that such changes as had occurred during the previous two decades tended to tighten, rather than loosen, gun controls in most parts of the world.

Notwithstanding some updating of the laws, patterns remain substantially the same. In democratic nations, possession of firearms is controlled by a permit system that varies in strictness from one country to another. In dictatorships, private ownership of firearms or explosives is forbidden to all but police and the military, a major exception allowing gun permits for hunting purposes only.

In many Asian, African and Latin American countries, crimes of violence often are carried out with knives, machetes or other "silent" weapons. This is also true of Italy, where the "arma blanca," or white weapon, continues to be the favorite instrument of individuals who have only a knife or other cutting weapon at hand. Such limitations do not affect organized criminal or terrorist groups like the Mafia in Italy, the Shining Path in Peru, the elusive international Red Brigades and the bevy of Middle East organizations that specialize in kidnapping and political killings. These groups have both the money and the connections to obtain weapons of all varieties.

Police state methods of control are often offered as evidence of a very low crime rate. As the press secretary of the People's Republic of China explained, "Crimes related to the use of weapons are rare since production and transaction [sale] of guns other than hunting guns are illegal."[2] Casualties resulting from police or military action against unarmed civilians—as in Tiananmen Square in June 1989—are not recorded as crimes, and of the thousands who died or were wounded or taken prisoner, only those who challenged or criticized the dictatorship were characterized as lawbreakers.

Japan, on the other hand, publishes comprehensive statistics on a wide variety of crimes, including those committed with firearms and other weapons. It also maintains a strict screening process for persons seeking permission to possess a gun. The government's approach to this problem is expressed in the following excerpts from a report provided by the Japanese embassy in Washington:

In Japan the possession of guns and swords is generally forbidden under the Law Controlling Possession, etc. of Firearms and Swords from the standpoint of public safety and security.

Permission must be obtained from the Prefectural [regional] Public Safety Commission to possess guns. Permission is denied to people under 18 years of age (people under 20 in the case of hunting guns), the mentally deranged, or drug addicts, those with no fixed abode, those with previous criminal records (in particular, those who have previously violated the Law Controlling Possession, etc. of Firearms and Swords), and *boryokudan* [gang] members who may possibly endanger public safety. Permission to possess a rifle is granted only to professional hunters or those who have possessed a hunting shotgun for 10 years or more.

With respect to handgun, its possession is subject to strictest control. Possession of such a gun is allowed only to police officers, Self-Defense personnel, or those who have been recognized by the Prefectural Public Safety Commission as pistol shooting contestants in international matches.

The possession of swords for hunting and fishing is authorized by the Prefectural Public Safety Commission as long as the purposes of their use are clearly defined.

The possession of other edged tools without any justifiable reason is prohibited.[3]

Statistically, the homicide rate in Japan is slightly under 1 per 100,000 persons, 1,308 such deaths being reported in 1989, when the total population was approximately 123 million.[4]

The greater detail available for 1987 shows that of the 51,174 felonies and other violent crimes reported that year, only 319 were committed with guns, "about 90 percent of which involved *boryokudan* members." The report adds that "the number of illegally possessed handguns which were seized in Japan in the course of 1987 totaled 1,592, most of which were possessed by *boryokudan* members and smuggled in from abroad."[5]

Not one of the eleven African governments canvassed in 1990 responded to this writer's inquiry. The *Washington Post's* 1968 survey singled out Kenya as typifying countries in which "governments are in firm control" and maintain the tightest kinds of restrictions on private possession of guns.[6] The nature of the limit of personal freedom that is exercised throughout Africa is spelled out in the annual volumes published by Freedom House, which as late as 1990 classified Kenya and most other countries on that continent as "not free."[7] In 1990 neither Kenya nor the normally more communicative governments of Egypt (partly free) and South Africa (not free) provided any information regarding their gun laws or crimes committed with guns. Considering the level of violence in those countries by both government security forces and political dissidents, their silence on this subject is understandable.

Equally silent—for much the same reason—were the governments of the Middle East. Israel, the only democratic country in that area, was as unresponsive as its neighbors. However, it makes no attempt to conceal the fact that its armed forces remain on a war footing in recognition of the continuing threat of attack by any of the Arab nations that still consider themselves at war with Israel. And despite the agreements reached in 1994 with the Palestine Liberation Organization and Jordan, it does not hesitate to grant gun permits to Israeli civilians in those occupied and border areas that are constantly subject to attack by Arabs who oppose the 1994 agreements and who continue their attacks either from within Gaza and the West Bank or by units operating out of Lebanon.

Elsewhere in that area, the Iran-Iraq War, the U.S.-Iraq War and unending civil wars in Afghanistan and Lebanon have put arms in the hands of countless numbers of people in those countries. And in wartime the only killings that are characterized as criminal are those perpetrated by "the enemy."

Among the nations of Latin America, the two most responsive to the 1990 canvass were Brazil and Chile, the former listed as free by Freedom House, the latter as "partly free," a classification granted only after dictator August Pinochet permitted an election to select a new president while he, Pinochet, kept control of the armed forces. Brazil's most severe restrictions apply to "arms, accessories, equipment and ammunitions equal or similar to material in use by the National or Foreign Armed Forces." This automatically excludes from private use all high-caliber pistols and rifles and all automatic or assault-type weapons. Brazilian authorities provided no data on criminal activity.[8]

A letter from the director general of the Policia de Investigaciones de Chile gave no regulatory information but did list the number of homicides involving the use of firearms during the years 1988–1991. The figures given were 117 for 1988, 135 in 1989, 136 in 1990 and 42 for the first three months of 1991.[9] These statistics must be viewed in light of this 1990 evaluation by Freedom House:

There was a surge of campaign-related violence in the months before the [1989] election. Nearly two dozen attacks against the offices of both the opposition Coalition and rightist parties were recorded, as well as close to a thousand arrests by police during confrontational political demonstrations.[10]

A year earlier, Freedom House had reported that even after Pinochet had agreed not to run for reelection to the presidency, "prisoners of conscience were still commonly taken for short periods; torture, political expulsion, internal exile, and assassination of government opponents continues."[11]

Some of the most interesting developments are seen in eastern Europe among countries formerly controlled from Moscow. With the collapse of the Soviet Union, adoption of a more open society in the remnants of its empire and the introduction of elements of free enterprise, access to firearms has become less difficult. Private possession of guns is less likely to bring automatic arrest and confiscation, even though the laws governing ownership remain strict. In Poland, for example, a law passed in 1961 still governs the sale of firearms, limiting them to members of the diplomatic corps and individuals who have police permits, principally for hunting weapons. However, under a 1990 order from the minister of internal affairs, permits may be issued by the regional police chief "if the circumstances claimed by the petitioner justify it." Restrictions similar to those in the United States preclude the sale of weapons to minors, mental patients, drug addicts and alcoholics, but include also persons "without permanent residence or steady source of income" as well as "the person suspected that he can use the firearm contrary to the safety of the State or contrary to the social system (order)." An unusual precaution is the requirement that the seller of a firearm must, in the presence of a police officer, fire three cartridges from the weapon before transferring ownership, and he must keep the shells with the record of sale. Presumably, the police keep the bullets for purposes of comparison with others found in any investigation of a crime, although the regulation doesn't so state. Statistics on crimes committed with firearms in Poland show a sharp increase in 1990 over the previous six years, but a decrease in the number of arrests for illegal possession of arms or ammunition.[12]

An interesting sidelight is provided by one of a series of "Dispatches from Eastern Europe" published in the *National Geographic* issue of March 1991, the same month in which the Polish director of the Institute of Justice released the information just discussed. A report from the magazine's correspondent in Poland includes these observations:

With the collapse of the police state, law and order have broken down. Cops are seldom seen, except halfheartedly directing traffic, and clearly they would just as soon not interfere in the lives of fellow citizens. As a result, a wave of burglaries, stickups, muggings, and murders is sweeping Eastern Europe. "Business is fantastic," says the young man running the gas-gun store [who] sells all kinds of gas weapons. Imported from West Germany, these pistols fire gas pellets: tear gas, temporarily paralyzing gas, asphyxiating gas, and skin-burning gas, all perfectly legal now, and perhaps some comfort to those who fear the crime wave. The most popular gun, at least among younger customers, is a heavy black model known as the "Miami," after the *Miami Vice* television program, a favorite in Poland.[13]

Although the magazine correspondent refers to gas guns as "perfectly legal," the regulations provided by Poland's Institute of

Justice state that the gas weapon is included in the term "firearm." However, the statistics included in that report do not include offenses committed with the use of gas guns, which suggests that their use is not considered as serious a violation as offenses committed with more lethal weapons.

Of the other members of the Warsaw Pact, only Czechoslovakia provided information on this subject. That country's 1983 law, as amended in 1990, established a permit system for private ownership of guns.[14] Administration and enforcement of the law, which deals with both weapons and ammunition, rests with the police, who are required to keep meticulous records of every purchase, sale or transfer and who are authorized to check at any time on the location, ownership or possession of guns.

Private ownership is limited principally to hunting weapons and ammunition for those weapons. A hunting license must be obtained and shown when applying for a gun permit. The application must be submitted to the police station in the jurisdiction in which the applicant resides. It must provide complete identification of the individual and the weapon desired, and must be accompanied by a statement from a physician certifying the mental health and competency of the applicant. Both hunting licenses and gun permits are valid for three years. When the gun permit expires, the owner must turn the weapon in until the permit is renewed. Any sale of a weapon by one individual to another must occur in the presence of the buyer, who must present a valid permit of his own.

Before a permit is renewed, the police have the right to see the gun, the ammunition held by the owner and the documents identifying both. They may also check to see whether present conditions are the same as those indicated by records already in their files. If there is not sufficient evidence in all the records to show this, "the police will make arrangements for their correction."[15] There will always be a follow-up to ensure that the appropriate correction has been made, and a note to that effect is put into the file on the gun's owner. Government information on illegal activity with a weapon in Czechoslovakia in 1990 and the first quarter of 1991 is provided in Table 7.1.

Two impressions of current conditions in Czechoslovakia were reported by a Czech citizen who fled from the country in 1988 and last visited the capital city of Prague in 1991. The first was a feeling of relief at the freedom of movement within the country experi-

Table 7.1
Illegal Activity with a Weapon in Czechoslovakia,
January 1990–March 1991

ACTIVITY	PISTOL	LONG GUN	KNIFE	OTHER
Murder	26	15	170	27
Robbery	38	1	125	64
Attack on Police Officer	5	3 (machine guns)	75	37
Harming Health of Another	19	17	669	145

Source: JUDr. Josef SVOBODA to author, 16 January 1991.

enced during the 1991 visit and the ease with which both entry and exit across the border were accomplished. A less comforting impression was that there is a flourishing trade in illegal weapons and a substantial rise in the crime rate, robbery in particular.[16] As in Poland, this appears to be due in part to the combination of inflation and unemployment that accompanies the conversion from a tightly controlled political and economic system to a democratic, open-market economy.

Appeals to the governments of western Europe brought a generally positive response. Information on gun-control laws and violations of those laws were obtained from the Federal Republic of [West] Germany, the Netherlands, Sweden, Switzerland and the United Kingdom.

Switzerland has what is probably the world's most completely armed population outside of Israel. The reason is clear from this introduction to a summary of Swiss gun controls supplied by the consulate general in New York:

Military service in Switzerland is compulsory and all male Swiss citizens incorporated in combatant militia units are taught how to shoot, beginning at age 20 with basic military training. Rifle clubs teach younger men how to shoot in voluntary preparatory courses. All combatant militia troops (ages 20 to 50) are obliged to keep their personal weapon, normally an automatic assault rifle, and ammunition at home.[17]

"Under no circumstances" may this weapon or ammunition be used for personal purposes. Any breach of that regulation makes the offending militiaman subject to imprisonment under "military criminal law."

Firearms purchased for private use are controlled by cantonal (state) law. The regulations vary from one canton to another, but unlike the situation in the United States, the cantons have joined in a "Concordat" under which all agree on these requirements: that commercial sellers of firearms be licensed and obligated to keep a record of every sale, which will include full identification of both the purchaser and the weapon purchased; that the individual buyer must obtain from the local police a "firearms purchase certificate," which will not be issued to "persons under 18 years of age, to mentally ill people, to persons under guardianship, to alcoholics, as well as to persons with a criminal record, or if a reasonable suspicion of doing harm with a weapon to themselves or third parties exists." A two-year permit may be issued to authorize "the carrying of handguns, gasguns, pointed weapons (such as daggers, etc.), blunt weapons (such as knuckledusters, etc.) as well as the transportation of these weapons in public transport facilities," but only "if danger to the applicant's person or property can be substantiated." Finally, "private ownership of machine pistols, machine guns, explosive weapons (i.e., hand grenades and bombs) as well as weapons simulating articles of daily use, is prohibited."[18]

The information on crime sent in response to my inquiry did not include statistics on crimes committed with guns. It did, however, show a total of 2,481 "criminal offenses against life and physical integrity" for 1987. What portion of that figure represents homicides is not indicated.[19]

The Netherlands Arms and Ammunition Act divides weapons into four categories. Category 1 includes "certain undesirable weapons" such as stilettos, switchblades, knuckle-dusters and bludgeons. Only members of the military are authorized to possess items of this sort. Category 2 features fully automatic firearms, heavy military weapons, silencers and explosives such as grenades and Molotov cocktails. Weapons in this group may be used by the military and police if they are "part of their regular equipment."[20]

Only Category 3 weapons, which consist of rifles, handguns, swords and knives, are available to the public, and then under severe restrictions. Hunters may obtain permits to possess guns, but they may "bear" them only to and from their homes and the hunting area. They are not permitted, as in many of the United States, to put their rifles or shotguns in racks in their cars or trucks and carry them wherever they go. Similarly, members of rifle clubs may qualify for ownership permits, but they must transport their weapons "wrapped," and only between home and the shooting range.

Category 4 has a tongue-in-cheek quality, but it is serious in its acknowledgment of the fact that "under special circumstances" ordinary household or sporting equipment may be "used to inflict injury: e.g. table legs, baseball bats." Used in that fashion, these items become weapons under the law. Statistics on the criminal use of firearms indicate that the number of such incidents rose sharply from 361 in 1983 to a peak of 705 in 1988, followed by a drop to 547 in 1989. Between 38 and 40 percent of these incidents were what the Dutch report as "shootouts." However, the number of deaths was remarkably low, averaging only 63 per year from 1986 to 1989. This translates to .43 per 100,000 population.[21]

Sweden publishes its entire penal code in English. In 1990 it also issued an English translation of an official report on crime in that country. Neither publication deals with regulations affecting gun ownership. However, the scale of punishments for crimes of violence suggests a remarkable degree of leniency where there is no intent to commit a crime. Consider, for example, Section 7 in Chapter 3 of the penal code:

A person who through carelessness causes the death of another shall be sentenced, *for causing another's death* to imprisonment for at most two years or, if the crime is petty, to pay a fine. If the crime is grave, imprisonment shall be imposed for at least six months and at most four years.[22]

One cannot help but wonder under what circumstances the crime of "causing another's death" could be considered petty.

Where intent is clear, "a person who takes the life of another shall be sentenced for murder to imprisonment for ten years or for life."[23] Under a conspiracy section, the person who hires another to commit a crime may suffer the same penalty as the one hired to do the job.[24]

An interesting social concept appears in a section of the code dealing with fines. Except where the law stipulates upper or lower limits, fines are imposed "proportional to the offender's daily income."[25] If applied in the United States—where such a law would probably be declared unconstitutional—this would permit fining the head of a major corporation a hundred times as much as one of the company's lowest paid employees for the same misdeed.

Violent crimes have risen steadily in number from fewer than 10,000 a year in the 1950s and 1960s to more than 38,000 in 1988. However, most of these were simple assaults. "Homicides, manslaughter and deadly assault," which increased only moderately during this period, accounted for 146 cases in 1988, less than .5 percent of the total and only 1.74 deaths per 100,000 population.[26] In this category the number of reported crimes is probably much closer to the actual number of incidents than records of nonlethal assaults, which the reporting agency freely admits may be three times as great as the number reported to the police.[27] The report contains no breakdown of crimes by type of weapon used, but a separate summary of "assault, robbery and rape by occurrence of weapons" in the capital city of Stockholm shows that of the 6,077 cases reported in 1987, 73 percent were carried out with no weapon of any kind, and only 221 (3.6 percent) involved the use of firearms. This represents nearly a threefold increase since 1970 in the number of crimes committed with firearms, and a doubling of the 1970 rate of 1.7 percent.[28]

A brief, nonstatistical summary supplied by the consulate of the Federal Republic of [West] Germany indicates that "regulations regarding fire arms and ammunition are very restrictive." Control is exercised by city police in the larger municipalities and by county authorities elsewhere. Special regulations provide that holders of U.S. hunting licenses who obtain "a German hunting invitation" may apply for "a 24-hour hunting license valid for a period of 14 consecutive days." Even the exporting of weapons is closely controlled. American citizens may purchase guns and ammunition in Germany only if they are to be delivered to the buyer's home address in the United States.[29]

The most complete information came from Great Britain and the principal members of the British Commonwealth: Canada, Australia and New Zealand. The Central Office of Information in London provided a brief history of twentieth-century British gun-control legislation, from the Firearms Act of 1920 down to the most recent effort to tighten controls, a 1988 statute that came into force the following year. Over that period, restrictions on the sale, possession and carrying of firearms became increasingly more strict, particularly during the 1960s, when the British experienced the same surge of what they term "hooliganism" that exploded in the United States.[30]

Currently, even a shotgun, long considered "a tool of the trade for the British farmer or gamekeeper," may not be purchased or possessed without a certificate issued by the police. Moreover, this commonly owned weapon may hold no more than two cartridges, which eliminates the multiple-shot pump gun and magazine-fed shotguns. Penalties for infractions of the law have been increased, especially for possession of "prohibited weapons," a category that includes machine guns, submachine guns, grenades, bombs, explosive bullets and rockets. A certificate will be issued for the purchase or possession of a rifle or pistol only if the police chief is satisfied that "an applicant has a good reason for possessing the weapon and is fit to be entrusted with it, and that the public safety or peace will not be endangered." Unlike the approach taken in many parts of the United States, British regulations state: "Personal protection is not regarded as a good reason for having a firearm."[31]

Penalties for criminal use of firearms in Great Britain are heavy. Life imprisonment may be imposed for "possessing a firearm with intent to endanger life, or using a firearm to resist arrest [or] possessing a firearm with criminal intent." Even without a showing of criminal intent, possessing a firearm without a certificate may be punished by imprisonment for up to three years "and/or an unlimited fine."[32] The maximum penalty of life imprisonment applies to the criminal use of imitation firearms as well. This means that a criminal using a toy pistol when committing an indictable offence may be treated as severely as one using a real weapon.

Recognizing the increasing tendency of diplomatic personnel to carry firearms for their own protection, the British nevertheless insist that "diplomats from other states stationed in London are bound to accept the British laws on the control of firearms."[33] Thus, representatives from countries like Poland, which exempts its diplomats from gun controls at home, are not afforded that privilege in Great Britain.

Britain's tightening of restrictions on firearms and the increasing severity of penalties for their use in criminal activity were a direct result of the growing incidence of violence and the use of guns in a land unaccustomed to this kind of weaponry in either private hands or as part of normal police equipment. In this respect the

British response has been more prompt, more forthright, and more effective than the few timid steps taken in the United States. For although the number of crimes committed with firearms in the British isles increased by almost 60 percent from 1978 to 1987, that number began to drop in 1988, the year new restrictions and new penalties were introduced. Moreover, the number of homicides in which firearms caused death averaged only forty-seven per year in all of England and Wales. If this rate were applied to the United States, which has a population five times that of Great Britain, the number of murders committed annually with firearms would be 235. As it is, murders in the United States commited with handguns alone averaged 9,200 each year during the decade in which those in Britain totalled 519 for the entire period.[34]

Notwithstanding its low homicide rate, one of Britain's most significant reactions to the increasing violence from criminals, terrorists and conflicting ethnic groups was to relax the earlier stringent rule against arming the police. While there is no inventory of firearms held by police units nationwide, it is known that some police are armed whenever they are on duty and others are issued weapons to meet particular dangers. One study of this policy reports that police who "regularly carry guns as a matter of routine . . . include the Royal and Diplomatic Protection Squads and possibly, for limited periods, the Robbery Squads." This practice is not limited to London. In the industrial city of Manchester, the chief constable disclosed in 1984 that "armed police were on regular patrol."[35]

More specific information is available as to the number of occasions in the early 1980s in which British police were issued guns. Considering the British tradition of unarmed police, the figures are startling: 7,275 in 1980, 6,149 in 1981 and 7,952 in 1982. More than three-quarters of these incidents occurred in London, and the figures do not include the arming of the protection squads mentioned above. The author of this 1985 study estimated that "about ten percent of the police officers in England and Wales are trained in the use of arms although the figure for the [London] Metropolitan Police is nearer twenty percent."[36] However, he points out that

some comfort may be gained from the fact that however many guns may be issued each year to the police, they are very seldom fired at people. Figures given to the writer by the Home Office indicate that guns were actually fired by the police in ten incidents in 1980, four incidents in 1981 and ten incidents in 1982.[37]

The infrequent use of firearms, as distinct from their issuance, results from the strictness of the "Guidelines for the Police on the Issue and Use of Firearms," which includes these basic principles:

- Firearms are to be issued only where there is reason to suppose that a police officer may have to face a person who is armed or otherwise so dangerous that he could not safely be restrained without the use of firearms.
- Firearms are to be used by authorized and trained police officers only as a last resort . . . for example, when it is apparent that a police officer cannot achieve the lawful purpose of preventing loss, or further loss, of life by any other means.
- Firearms should be issued only to officers who have been trained and authorized in a particular class of weapon.[38]

The guidelines close with this warning:

- The responsibility for the USE of the firearm is an INDIVIDUAL decision which may have to be justified in legal proceedings. REMEMBER THE LAW. REMEMBER YOUR TRAINING.[39]

Other members of the British commonwealth were equally forthcoming with information regarding their gun laws and infractions of those laws. The volumes of material supplied by Canada, Australia and New Zealand demonstrate the seriousness with which those countries view this problem.

A pamphlet published by the Canadian Department of Justice after major changes in gun-control sections of the criminal law were made in 1977 is subtitled *Working Together to Save Lives*. Three objectives of the new laws are given:

1. to reduce the criminal use of guns:
2. to keep guns out of the hands of dangerous persons:
3. to encourage and ensure responsible gun ownership and use.[40]

To obtain these objectives the courts are authorized to prohibit ownership of firearms by criminals and "dangerous persons" and to impose heavier penalties for gun-related offenses. Police are given wide search-and-seizure powers, subject to subsequent justification. And severe restrictions are placed on ownership of weapons "not considered reasonable for hunting or sporting purposes," with an absolute ban on possession of "prohibited weapons" such as sawed-off shotguns and rifles and fully automated weapons. Finally, a Firearms Acquisition Certificate (FAC) is made a requisite for anyone wishing to obtain a firearm of any kind.

In submitting an application, the prospective gun owner is required to provide, in addition to information as to his age, address, occupation, physical description, and so forth, answers to the following questions:

a) Have you been convicted of an indictable criminal offense associated with violence for which a pardon has not been granted?
b) Have you, during the past five years, been treated for a mental disorder which was associated with violence or threatened or attempted violence on your part, whether against yourself or another person?
c) Have you been prohibited from possessing a firearm, ammunition or explosive substance?
d) Have you been refused a Firearms Acquisition Certificate, Restricted Weapon Registration Certificate, or firearms permit?
e) Have you had a Restricted Weapon Certificate or firearms permit revoked?
f) Have you completed a course in, or successfully completed a test related to the safe handling and use of firearms?[41]

A three-year study of the effectiveness of the new laws was conducted by an independent organization, which published its final report in 1983. The study revealed that although murders had increased steadily through the fifteen years prior to enactment of the 1977 legislation, they "consistently declined since that time." An examination of attempted murders in four of the country's largest cities showed "a decline in the proportion of these incidents committed with firearms in the post-legislative period compared to pre-1978."[42]

Drawing upon data contained in this study, Canada's solicitor general issued a summary that began with a comparison between Canadian and U.S. experience during the first year of the Reagan presidency. Citing FBI Uniform Crime Reports, the review charted the 20,053 murders in the United States and 599 in Canada to point up two facts: the murder rate of 8.8 per 1,000 population in the United States compared with 2.48 in Canada; the percentage of murders committed by firearms, which was 62 percent in the United States, was 29 percent in Canada. Canadian statistics show that even the percentage of robberies committed with firearms dropped from the 1977 level of 38.5 to 34.4 in 1981. A sharper decrease occurred in the number of accidental deaths by firearms.[43] Equally significant is a statistic that shows 50 percent of American fatalities having been produced by handguns, compared with 10 percent of Canadian deaths. The report acknowledges that these differences may have influenced public opinion in which, according to a 1982 Gallup poll, 70 percent of Canadian respondents supported even more severe restrictions on firearms than those imposed by the 1977 legislation.[44]

The demand for further stiffening of gun controls was strenuously resisted by the National Firearms Association—Canada's version of the National Rifle Association.[45] Nevertheless, by October 1991 legislation was approved by Parliament to raise the minimum age for acquiring firearms from 16 to 18, establish a 28-day waiting period for screening every individual applying for a Firearms Acquisition Certificate (FAC), require successful completion of a firearms safety training course before a FAC can be issued, determine that permit fees must cover the cost of FAC program administration, require collectors to "demonstrate knowledge of the characteristics of firearms to be collected" and consent to periodic inspections, tighten control over military and paramilitary weapons, and increase the maximum sentences for violation of the law from five to ten years for a first conviction and "from 10 years to life for repeated convictions."[46]

In Australia each state has its own laws governing firearms and has the option of adopting relevant national laws that are designed for the Australian Capital Territory. Currently, two of the seven states and territories use the national weapons licensing system that was established in 1937. Under that system, police, armed forces personnel, local government departments, rangers and National Rifle Association members are exempt from the licensing provisions. A Weapons Bill, introduced in 1990, which would tighten the restrictions on private ownership and the use of military-type weapons, is being strongly resisted by gun dealers and clubs.[47]

Among Australia's states, licensing laws vary, both in their terms and in the level of difficulty the applicant faces in obtaining approval. Permits for the use of "long arms"—principally rifles and shotguns—are reasonably easy to secure in all states except relatively densely populated Victoria. Queensland and Tasmania require no permit for possession of these commonly used hunting weapons. Pistol permits are harder to obtain everywhere, and in most jurisdictions they must be renewed every year, whereas rifle owners need reapply only every three years. In every state, permits are issued by the police, and only after they determine that the applicant is a "fit and proper" person to entrust with a weapon.[48]

More centralized is New Zealand's control of firearms under the Arms Act of 1983 and regulations issued in 1984 when the act went into effect. Although hunting is as traditional there as in Australia, New Zealand does not exempt members of its National Rifle Association from firearms regulations. Even among government departments, exemptions are only for members of the armed forces, police and the two agencies responsible for scientific research and government stores.

Throughout New Zealand's Arms Act, the term "fit and proper person" is used as a general qualification for anyone applying for a gun license, whether that person is seeking to establish a dealership or merely to purchase a weapon. The term "fit and proper" is not defined in either the law or administrative regulations, its application being left entirely to the discretion of the police who issue the licenses and enforce the law. Dealers are so closely supervised that they must "at all times permit any member of the Police to inspect and make copies of any entries in the book" kept as a record of purchases and sales. They must also allow police to inspect, without prior warning, their business premises and any of their weapons.[49] Warrants for seizure of a dealer's weapons are issued by the Commissioner of Police and may be executed with the use of "such force as may be necessary." Importation of weapons is by permit only, with violators "liable on summary conviction to imprisonment for a term not exceeding 1 year or to a fine not exceeding 2,000 pounds, or to both."[50]

As with dealers, prospective purchasers of weapons must be fit and proper persons, as determined by police in the locality in which the purchase is to be made. That phrase is repeated over and over again in Section 24 of the act governing individual purchases and in implementing regulations as well.

Special permission is required for purchase or possession of a pistol, a privilege that is granted only to dealers, members of recognized pistol shooting clubs, and individually identified employees of museums, broadcasting companies and moving picture companies. Pistol owners must not only provide detailed personal information to obtain a permit, they must notify the police of any change of address and any plan to take the pistol out of the country.[51]

Equally tight control is maintained over "restricted weapons." Most notable in this section of the statute is the provision that this term "means any weapon, whether firearm or not, declared by the Governor General . . . to be a restricted weapon." The delegation of authority to an official of the executive branch of government avoids the loophole that the law opens when it attempts to define such weapons in specific terms that manufacturers or owners can avoid by making minor alterations in a proscribed weapon. Thus, if any attempt is made to circumvent the intent of the regulations by modifying or redesigning one of the weapons listed there, the list can be revised by the governor general at any time. As the list stands today it includes machine carbines or guns, submachine guns, both commercial and homemade grenades and grenade launchers, rockets and rocket launchers, and machine pistols "of any kind whatsoever."[52]

New Zealanders have few excuses for being ignorant of either their gun-control laws or the proper way to handle guns. A 54-page booklet, issued to every new gun owner by the New Zealand police, provides detailed information on the various kinds of firearms that may be purchased legally, the kinds of ammunition that can be used in each weapon—and the kinds that may not be used—plus many illustrated pages demonstrating both proper and improper uses of guns. The manual concludes with a list of dos and don'ts dictated either by government regulation or a sensible regard for the safety of the shooter and anyone in his vicinity.[53]

The care with which the New Zealand government approaches this problem is evident from statistics on death and injury from firearms. Over the seven-year period from 1978 to 1984, the number of murders committed with firearms ranged from 7 to 12 annually, with an average of 8.4. Using the standard measure of deaths per 100,000 population, the homicide rate in that country comes to 0.26, compared with 2.0 in Great Britain, 5.5 in Canada, and 8.4 in the United States.[54]

8

The Propaganda Campaign,
Pro and Con: Phase 1

By the 1960s the combination of drug use and violent crime had aroused pro- and anti-gun-control advocates alike. Of the ten most important domestic problems identified by Gallup pollsters in 1965, reducing the amount of crime was second only to improving public education.[1] Fear for personal safety and a feeling that the courts were not being harsh enough with criminals stirred both sides on the gun issue, one to urge tighter controls over the distribution of weapons, the other to propose doing away with controls but increasing the penalties for illegal use of weapons.

Demands for federal gun legislation, fueled by the assassination of President John F. Kennedy, made this an appropriate subject for the poll takers to follow. On the matter of gun permits, as in the past, more than two-thirds of those asked, and more than half of the gun owners who were questioned, favored requiring a police permit for the purchase of a gun. The propermit majority rose to 73 percent in 1967.[2] When in mid-1968 the pollsters' question was about what should be done to stop the violence, stricter gun laws took first place over stricter law enforcement.[3]

The assassination of Senator Robert Kennedy in 1968 and the public outcry that followed brought the subject close to home for members of Congress, who were deluged with mail urging passage of a federal law to curb the sale of firearms. One newspaper columnist quoted a European friend who asked, "Why are Americans so fond of guns? Is it their sexual immaturity?" Psychologists, the writer said, confirm the belief that a gun can be a sex symbol which, for some men, "bolsters their sense of masculinity."[4]

The counterattack was led by the NRA, whose president, Harold W. Glassen, denounced at a news conference what he called the "mass attempt" to "disarm American citizens." He further charged that in advising voters to petition Congress for stronger gun control, Senator Joseph D. Tydings of Maryland was party to a conspiracy "to deceive the American population into believing it should abrogate the Second Amendment to the Constitution."[5] In a letter to the NRA's 900,000 adult members, Glassen warned that the right of sportsmen to possess and use firearms "for proper lawful purposes is in the greatest jeopardy in the history of the country." Possibly having in mind an earlier NRA official's boast that his organization could generate "half a million letters to Congressmen within 72 hours," Glassen concluded by suggesting that members "clearly express their views without delay to their senators and congressmen."[6]

In Congress, several bills were under consideration. One favored by President Lyndon Johnson would prohibit mail-order purchases of long guns (rifles and shotguns used principally for hunting) and would establish controls over interstate commerce in ammunition. A similar bill had previously been killed in committee in the Senate. Of greater concern to Mr. Glassen was the Tydings bill, which would require all firearms to be registered and all prospective buyers to obtain a license prior to purchasing either guns or ammunition. Pulling out all stops in a second interview, Glassen introduced the spectre of communist influence, saying, "I do know that all Communist-front groups support gun bills. Their point is, 'We've got our guns, let's take the others'." "[7] The only compromise he was willing to make was to give his support to a curb on mail-order sales of handguns, a position the NRA would reverse in years to come.

President Johnson set the stage for passage of federal legislation that he had been urging for several years, in particular, a bill approved by the House in 1967. In a January 1968 award ceremony, he told members of the Twelfth Air Force, "There is not more urgent business before this Congress than to pass the Safe Streets Act this year that I proposed last year."[8] He made the same point later that month in his annual budget message to Congress, again in a February conversation with AFL-CIO President George Meany, and finally in a special message to Congress urging passage of the act (H.R. 5037), which combined requests for stronger criminal laws and a law that would "stop what amounts to mail order murder." Asking funds for 100 additional assistant U.S. attorneys, 100 additional FBI agents, and research and training grants for local police units, he added,

Once again I urge the Congress to enact the bill I proposed last year to:

- Prohibit interstate mail order sales and shipments of firearms, except between Federal licensees.
- Prohibit over-the-counter sales of handguns to out-of-state purchasers.
- Regulate the sale of firearms to minors.
- Further regulate the importation of firearms into this country.[9]

Passed by the House of Representatives in 1967, H.R. 5037 was stalled in the Senate until the spring of 1968, when it was approved by a vote of 72 to 4, with 24 not voting,[10] although with a number of amendments that aroused serious opposition when the bill was returned to the House. The debate that followed reflected both personal and local preferences as often as party loyalty. Democratic Representative Joe Waggoner of Louisiana was at odds with Emanuel Celler of Brooklyn, New York, over Senate changes regarding permissible police procedure that Celler said were constitutionally questionable. Waggoner responded, "It should be no more difficult for him [Celler] to accommodate himself to the wishes of what I believe to be the overwhelming majority of this House than it was for me to surrender some of the grave constitutional reservations which I had held regarding title VIII of the Civil Rights Act of 1968."[11]

Republican support of Waggoner's acceptance of the Senate's amendments was expressed by Representative Robert McClory of Illinois, who defended the changes as essential to stronger law enforcement. "Reluctant" support came from Democrat Joseph Karth of Minnesota, who thought the amended bill was weak in its gun-control section. "I feel strongly," he said, "that registration of firearms, like registration of automobiles, should be part of the permanent law."[12]

McClory's argument did not impress Democrats Henry Reuss of Wisconsin and Don Edwards of California, Reuss describing the Senate amendments as "patently unconstitutional" in their loosening of the rules to permit "indiscriminate wiretapping" and other police procedures that would undermine the Supreme Court's decisions regulating the admissibility of confessions and eyewitness testimony.[13]

In the end, the choice was between returning the bill to the House-Senate conference committee, which might well wind up in a deadlock, or accepting the measure with the Senate amendments. Under the lash of publicity and President Johnson's repeated demands for action, both parties in the House voted overwhelmingly to approve the amended bill.[14]

President Johnson's statement when he signed the Omnibus Crime Control and Safe Streets Act of 1968 highlighted two points: that it had taken three years to bring to fruition some aspects of the plan he had had in mind when he appointed a national crime commission in 1965, and that the bill finally passed by Congress was not enough to solve "the immediate crisis of local law enforcement." Calling the prohibition of interstate traffic in handguns "only a halfway step toward the protection of our families and homes," he challenged Congress to go on to pass the bill he was submitting to apply the same restrictions to rifles and shotguns. "We must close a glaring loophole in the law," he said, "by controlling the sale of these lethal weapons, as well as the sale of ammunition for all guns."[15]

Compromising on one point by adopting the view that the rules of evidence prescribed in the Crime Control Act could be interpreted "in harmony with the Constitution," he insisted that the loopholes opened by the wiretapping and electronic eavesdropping provisions went "far beyond the effective and legitimate needs of law enforcement."[16] His proposed gun-control bill would repeal this portion of the Crime Control Act.

Congress had spent sixteen months deliberating the pros and cons of crime control. Faced with a presidential demand for action on gun control that it had been unwilling to take in June, but which was clearly supported by public opinion, it went to work on Johnson's proposal in July.[17] Three months later it passed the Gun Control Act of 1968.

This was not accomplished without spirited debate. Emanuel Celler introduced the new bill (H.R. 17735) as one that could subject rifles, shotguns and ammunition to the same control as had been applied to handguns in the Crime Control Act. In essence, importation or interstate transportation of these weapons and other explosive devices would be forbidden except between licensed manufacturers and dealers. The bill did not include those modifications in police procedure recommended by President Johnson. Citing support for this legislation by the FBI, the President's Commission on Law Enforcement and the International Association of Chiefs of Police, Celler called attention to the fact that since 1900 more civilian deaths had been caused by firearms than all the deaths suffered "in all our wars from the Revolution to date." Acknowledging that protection of the individual was primarily a local police function, he pointed to the way in which states with strong gun-control laws were frustrated by the unhindered traffic in weapons from other states having little or no control. As an example, he noted that a recent survey showed that in Massachusetts, which requires a permit to purchase a handgun, "over 85 percent of weapons used in murders and holdups had been purchased in Maine and New Hampshire." This situation, which is found in other parts of the country as well, points up the need for federal intervention, which Celler said is simply this:

The reason that State gun laws do not work even better is that Federal law did not buttress State efforts to restrict gun acquisition. Former Federal law undercut State regulation by allowing guns to be purchased by mail order or across State lines. It is to restrict such interstate traffic in both long guns and ammunition that H.D. 17735 is directed.[18]

Republican William McCullock of Ohio controlled the "equal time" given the members of his party. However, as debate on the Crime Bill had demonstrated, this was not a party squabble. McCullock himself supported the administration's gun-control bill. On the other hand, Democrat Arnold Olsen of Montana expressed the anticontrol position as passionately as any NRA officer. "I cannot vote for the gun control legislation presently before the [H]ouse," he said, explaining:

I say this legislation will not work and gun control proponents will want more next year or the next year and they will not be satisfied with anything less than confiscation. I doubt even then that legislation can keep firearms out of the hands of criminals. . . . Surely we are dreaming if we think legislation such as this will be obeyed by the criminal element. It would be by the good citizens—farmers, ranchers, and sportsmen—who would suffer most if strong gun controls are enacted. Many of the people in our State of Montana keep firearms out of necessity. Ranchers and farmers use them in their daily work. Many of our citizens live in isolated areas far removed from the police protection which is available in urban centers.[19]

Insisting that the need for gun control varies from state to state, Olsen said he would support an amendment that would enable each state to adopt legislation "suited to their particular needs."[20]

Democrat Bob Casey of Texas also felt that the bill would harm only law-abiding citizens. Using time allotted by Celler, Casey called instead for a law that would exact tougher penalties on criminals who "do not stay in prison long enough now for the psychologists and the rehabilitation men to shake hands with them before they are out on the street again." His solution was a mandatory ten-year sentence for a first offense and twenty-five years for any subsequent offense for anyone who "uses or carries a firearm, which has been transported in interstate or foreign commerce, during commission of any robbery, assault, murder, rape, burglary, kidnaping, or homicide—other than involuntary manslaughter."[21]

Casey got part of his wish when the House voted overwhelmingly for an amendment that, although it would not delete control over interstate transportation of weapons, would mandate a 1 to 10 year sentence for the first felony offense with a weapon and 5 to 15 years for any subsequent offense, with no suspended sentence or probation permitted. With that major addition, the House passed the bill by close to a three to one majority.[22]

As in the House, the most serious opposition came from senators representing relatively sparsely populated states whose major interests were farming and ranching. Eleven of the seventeen negative votes were cast by senators from Arizona, Arkansas, the Dakotas, Idaho, Montana, Nevada and Wyoming. The remaining six were from southern states. But as the bill's chief sponsor, Thomas Dodd of Connecticut, pointed out, passage by a four to one majority was not a partisan matter and could not have been achieved without the help of senators "on both sides of the aisle."[23] Nevertheless, what had been approved was an amended version of the House bill that required referring the problem to a House-Senate conference committee. When the conference committee reported that its members had agreed to recommend the bill as amended by the Senate, a new dispute arose in the House. The changes that angered anticontrol House members were set forth in a comparative summary by Democrat Robert Sikes of Florida. These included the following: a ban on interstate transportation (mail order) of all ammunition, including that for rifles and shotguns, which had been excluded by the House; authorization allowing the secretary of the treasury "to define the scope of the provision [re licensing of collectors] by regulation"; a 7-day wait required for long gun purchases from neighboring states and an affidavit to be filed with the local law enforcement agency; elimination of the mandatory minimum sentence for first felony offence and "no requirement for consecutive terms in addition to terms for the base felony."[24] Sikes was joined by Democrat John Dingell of Michigan in denouncing these changes. Their ire was directed in particular at what they regarded as authority of the treasury secretary to "set aside, rewrite or add to the law virtually at will" and at penalty provisions that indicated greater concern for the rights of criminals than for those of law-abiding citizens.

On this last point they were joined by Republican Richard Poff of Virginia, who argued that great damage had been done by deletion of the requirement that the sentence for using a weapon should be added to the term assessed for the base felony (assault, murder, etc.) rather than served concurrently. Republican John Saylor of Pennsylvania agreed, declaring that if those deletions were accepted by the House, "there will be joy in the hearts of the criminals in America and . . . the law-abiding citizen, the hunter, the marksman, the trapshooter, the individuals who have from time immemorable in this country had shells available as a service to their patrons will be angry."[25]

Due to disapppointment with the committee's conclusion that this was the best compromise they could make, the number of supporters in the House dropped off sharply. Although the conference report was finally agreed to by a vote of 161 to 129, some 141 members were recorded as "not voting."[26] Signing the bill into law, President Johnson expressed his appreciation for the efforts of those who gave their support, but he said the act fell short of the objectives he had set in that it failed to include national registration of all guns and licensing of everyone who carried a gun. Without referring to the NRA or any other organization by name, he was blunt in stating that these measures had been blocked by "a powerful gun lobby."[27] He made no mention of the fact that the new law did not close the wiretapping loopholes that he felt should have been eliminated from the earlier Crime Control Act.

Although the fear professed by Senator Olsen that ultimately government would confiscate all guns was never shown to be the goal of any reputable gun-control organization or faction, this point continued to be argued in the perennial battle for and against tighter controls. A contributor to the *New York Times* wrote in 1972 that there seemed to be a growing belief that "a total ban on or extremely stringent control over firearms, particularly handguns, would reduce violent crime." This premise, the writer asserted, was based on two assumptions: "that all firearms owners are criminals [and] all crimes are committed with legally purchased weapons."[28] No evidence was offered to support either the initial premise or the two assumptions. An examination of the literature distributed by organizations like Handgun Control and the National Coalition to Ban Handguns reveals no such assumptions. As to handguns, the *New York Times* later pointed out that while the 1968 gun-control law banned imports of these weapons, it established no barrier to the importation of gun parts, and government statistics showed imports of handgun parts from 1969 through 1972 in sufficient quantities to permit the assembling of over 4 million "Saturday night specials." The report went on to say that a bill to close that loophole had been passed by the Senate, 65 to 25, but had been blocked in the House by the same Emanuel Celler who had been instrumental in getting congressional approval for the Gun Control Act of 1968. Calling the members of his Judiciary Committee "very gun conscious," Celler was clearly reacting to the NRA's reminder to its members that every representative in the House had to stand for reelection in November of that year (1972).[29]

Despite this setback, the struggle for stricter controls continued, the rising incidence of crimes involving guns spurring the introduction of new measures in every session of Congress. In 1975, fifty-one gun-control bills were put into the congressional hopper. One submitted on four separate occasions by New York's Democratic Representative Jonathan Bingham would have banned "the importation, manufacture, sale, purchase, transfer, receipt, possession, or transportation of handguns, except for or by members of the Armed Forces, law enforcement officials, and as authorized by the Secretary of the Treasury, licensed importers, manufacturers, dealers, antique collectors and pistol clubs."[30] This became the subject of a radio debate between Bingham and an attorney for the Federation of Greater New York Rifle and Pistol Clubs in which the usual question of Second Amendment rights was raised. Subsequently, a letter written by a retired officer of the NRA, circulated not only to NRA members but to thousands of nonmembers as well, quoted Bingham as acknowledging that his bill would require a revision of the Second Amendment. What Bingham actually said was that if his bill was ruled unconstitutional by the courts, he would take the alternate route and propose a constitutional amendment.[31]

A more spectacular charge in the NRA letter was that top-level New York City officials had "publicly advocated that all firearms be taken away from the city's patrolmen."[32] Undocumented and ludicrous as this statement was, it purported to justify the letter's suggestion that every reader send two enclosed postcards to his senators to let them know his opinion of gun control. The effectiveness of this campaign can only be inferred from the fact that all of the gun-control bills submitted to the House that year died in committee.

A similar fate met measures proposed by the Senate. These ranged from Hawaiian Republican Hiram Fong's bill to ban Saturday night specials to Idaho Republican James McClure's bill to repeal the entire Gun Control Act of 1968.[33] Unlike their counterparts in the House, where bills were submitted without comment and referred automatically to the Judiciary Committee, Fong and McClure took advantage of the unlimited speech privilege afforded by the Senate to explain the purposes of their proposals. Representing a strong-control state, Senator Fong made the point that "Saturday night specials have no legitimate sporting use nor any valid defense purpose." He would require a purchaser to appear in person "at the licensee's premises" to clearly establish his identity, then wait "at least 14 days" for his name to be checked with the local police and FBI.[34] McClure's comments included the following:

[T]he Gun Control Act of 1968 remains on the books as an example of a dangerous threat to the basic constitutional right of every American—the right to bear arms. [It is] a law passed at a moment of national hysteria [and] has proved to have no adverse affect on anyone other than the law-abiding citizen, while the crime statistics continue to rapidly rise.[35]

Because the issue continued to be hotly debated, it was occasionally raised in presidential news conferences. However, no president from Richard Nixon to Jimmy Carter showed any enthusiasm for the subject. After the attempted assassination of Alabama Governor George C. Wallace in 1972, President Nixon told a reporter, "I have always felt there should be a Federal law for the control of handguns . . . Saturday night specials." But he had not suggested including such a provision in the Organized Crime Control Act, which he signed in 1970, and he offered no assistance in getting such a law passed in 1972.[36]

The following year, after Mississippi Senator John C. Stennis had been shot, a reporter remarked to the president, "The White House has not spoken out very strongly against gun controls, particularly handguns," and asked whether the shooting had given Nixon any second thoughts. Repeating his earlier statement regarding the desirability of legislation to deal with Saturday night specials, the president added, "I have never hunted in my life. I have no interest in guns. . . . I am not interested in the National Rifle Association. . . . [T]he legislation that was originally suggested [by Hiram Fong] did not get through [the] Senate. . . . I have asked the Attorney General to give us a legislative formula . . . that can get through Congress."[37] If his attorney general ever devised such a formula, there is no evidence that it was communicated from the White House to Congress.

President Ford was equivocal on the subject of Saturday night specials, but he stated flatly, "I am not going to recommend the registration of owners . . . of guns, or handguns." Later in 1975 he told a reporter, "I did recommend to Congress early this year a rather comprehensive approach to crime control, a new proposal that would make it much more difficult to get what we call Saturday night specials." He did not enlarge on this aspect of his plan except to say that he had also proposed more severe penalties for criminal use of guns and mandatory sentences.[38]

These suggestions were incorporated into bills that committees in both House and Senate approved in the spring of 1976. But neither measure ever reached the floor for debate by the entire Congress because a ban on small, concealable handguns in the House version brought on what Democratic Representative John Seiberling of Ohio called the NRA's "most blatant lobbying campaign I have ever seen." That drive to derail the House bill intimidated enough members of the House Judiciary Committee to bring about a reversal of the 24 to 18 vote that had approved bringing the measure before the whole House. A new vote to return the bill to a subcommittee for further consideration passed, 17 to 16. The bill's sponsor, Democrat Martin Russo of Illinois, acknowledged that this action killed all gun-control legislation for the balance of that presidential election year.[39]

As election day approached, "The Great American Gun War" became the subject of a lengthy magazine article by a member of the conservative Hudson Institute whose only other identification in that journal was that he was "not a member of the National Rifle Association." This disclaimer notwithstanding, the writer's introduction, which attributed the phrase "gun lobby" to "a hostile media," set the tone of the article, in which the author's marshalling of statistics and anecdotes to prove the ineffectiveness of gun control legislation should have cheered anticontrol enthusiasts greatly.[40]

One of the article's conclusions—that nasty things may happen if and when gun owners feel trapped in an issue "kept at white heat"[41]—seemed prophetic the very next year. In April 1977, the president of the Federation of Greater New York Pistol and Rifle Clubs let it be known that he was offering a $200 reward to anyone who, in defense against an assault or robbery, shoots and kills his assailant. Although New York City's mayor and police commissioner were appalled by what Mayor Abraham Beame called "a thoroughly sickening" proposal, there was no suggestion that the offer would subject its originator to any kind of legal action.[42]

Not for the first time, the subject of gun control was important enough to be included in the Democratic and Republican platforms in 1976, but with a somewhat different approach from that taken in 1968. That earlier year, which produced the Gun Control Act, saw both parties pledging to "promote the passage and enforcement of effective federal, state and local gun control legislation" (Democratic platform), or "enactment of legislation to control indiscriminate availability of firearms, safeguarding the right of responsible citizens to collect, own and use firearms for legitimate purposes" (Republican platform). This theme was repeated in the 1972 presidential platforms, with emphasis on "cheap, readily-obtainable handguns" (Republican) or "Saturday night specials" (Democratic). In 1976, however, the Democratic platform attempted to appeal to both sides, while the Republicans turned to a completely anticontrol position. The full statement of each party was as follows:

[Democratic platform:] Handguns simplify and intensify violent crime. Ways must be found to curtail the availability of these weapons. The Democratic Party must provide the leadership for a coordinated federal and state effort to strengthen the presently inadequate controls over the manufacture, assembly, distribution and possession of handguns and to ban Saturday night specials.

Furthermore, since people and not guns commit crimes, we support mandatory sentencing for individuals convicted of committing a felony with a gun.

The Democratic Party, however, affirms the right of sportsmen to possess guns for purely hunting and target shooting purposes.

[Republican platform:] We support the right of citizens to keep and bear arms. We oppose federal registration of firearms. Mandatory sentences for crimes committed with a lethal weapon are the only effective solution to this problem.[43]

The battle was renewed in 1978 when Carter's Treasury Department attempted to improve its ability to trace guns used in crimes by regulations calling for individual identification of every new gun by manufacturer, model, caliber and number; for quarterly reports of all purchases and sales by dealers and for reports of all thefts within 24 hours. A request for $4.2 million to implement the program brought Congress into the picture and produced a stream of protests against what Republican Representative Steven Symm of Idaho told the House was "the first step toward gun control." A countercampaign in support of the regulations by the National Coalition to Ban Handguns made no impression on either Congress or reporters, who wrote only of the influence exerted by the National Rifle Association. The House Appropriations Committee responded by cutting $4.2 million from the Treasury Department budget. When this was put to a vote on the floor, the cut was approved, 314 to 80.[44]

A year later the officers of Handgun Control, Inc., charged President Carter with backing away from his campaign promise to support stricter regulation of firearms and turned to Democratic Senator Edward Kennedy for assistance. The National Coalition joined the fray with a circular letter asking people to write Kennedy and ask for "any legislation that will control hand-guns and eliminate carnage." NCBH also listed in its newsletter the names of 175 representatives and 22 senators who had accepted campaign contributions ranging from $50 to $9,800 from the NRA, the Gun Owners of America, and the Citizens Committee for the Right to Keep and Bear Arms. That this effort was doomed to failure was indicated in a news report that recalled the gun lobby's successful blocking of the Treasury Department's proposed regulations and added that the same pressure group had been responsible for preventing Senate confirmation of President Carter's nominee to head the Law Enforcement Assistance Administration.[45]

9

Propaganda: Phase 2

Prior to 1980, presidents from Johnson to Carter had blown hot and cold on the subject of gun control. Of this group only Johnson took a firm stand in favor of restrictions imposed at the national level. Without his outspoken public position and his prodding of Congress, there would have been no Gun Control Act of 1968. Nixon and Ford acknowledged the danger posed by the proliferation of Saturday night specials, but they did not go out of their way to push control legislation.

President Carter initially expressed himself in favor of federal controls but backed off when faced with serious opposition from a Congress that, even among Democrats, viewed him as an outsider. He was also well aware that only a year before his election, despite what the Democratic chairman of the House Judiciary Committee saw as a public "screaming for something to be done," Representative Jonathan Bingham of New York had failed to get congressional approval for a bill to prohibit the importation, manufacture, sale, purchase, transfer, receipt, possession or transportation of handguns, a bill in which he made exceptions only for the police, armed forces and licensed manufacturers, dealers, collectors and pistol clubs.[1] Moreover, Carter was more concerned about other problems that would be unmanageable without the cooperation of Congress.

The 1980 election changed all that; President Reagan entered Washington as the John Wayne of the White House, proud of his

membership in the National Rifle Association and equally enthusiastic in expressing the macho vision he had of his country,
which he capsuled as "the 'A-Team' among nations."[2] His opposition to gun-control laws was unaffected by the attempt on his life,
which occurred in his third month in office. Three weeks later, in
his first meeting with reporters, he was asked if the attempted
assassination had changed his thinking about gun control. His
answer was one he held to throughout his eight years in office:
Laws against possession of a gun are unenforceable; we're showing
the results of several decades of growing permissiveness, unwill-
ingness to hold individuals responsible for their misdeeds, blaming
society instead, and "what we need is quicker, more effective
justice." He expanded on this at a formal news conference, citing
California law as more realistic than the federal statute in its use of
a mandatory additional penalty of from "5 to 15 years to the prison
sentence for anyone carrying a gun in the commission of a crime."[3]

While this description of the California law was not complete—
omitting the fact that it requires a waiting period before purchase
of a handgun—it was an accurate reflection of Reagan's 1980
platform, which included the following statement:

We [Republicans] believe the right of citizens to keep and bear arms must
be preserved. Accordingly, we oppose federal registration of firearms.
Mandatory sentences for commission of armed felonies are the most
effective means to deter abuse of this right. We therefore support congressional initiatives to remove those provisions of the Gun Control Act of
1968 that do not significantly impact on crime but serve rather to restrain
the law-abiding citizen in his legitimate use of firearms.[4]

The Democratic position was stated with equal frankness:

The Democratic Party affirms the right of sportsmen to possess guns for
purely hunting and target-shooting purposes. However, handguns
simplify and intensify violent crime. Ways must be found to curtail the
availability of these weapons. The Democratic Party supports enactment
of federal legislation over the manufacture, assembly, distribution, and
possession of handguns and to ban Saturday night specials.[5]

As the 1980 election drew near, *Congressional Quarterly* noted in
its weekly newsletter that a young gun-control lobby had been
able to raise only $6,300 for candidates it believed would support
its position. This, the editor observed, was a drop in the bucket

compared to the campaign contributions made by progun organizations, which had spent $180,000 just to help defeat Edward Kennedy's bid for the Democratic presidential nomination. In the face of this kind of power, the newsletter reported, even some liberal Democrats had turned tail and signed up as cosponsors of one of the bills backed by the NRA.[6]

Despite the procontrol policy adopted by the party's leadership, there were Democrats who were opposed to gun legislation for the same reasons as those of the NRA. Representative Allen Ertel of Pennsylvania defended his anticontrol position in this fashion:

My views on the issue are based on my experience, as a prosecutor, with Pennsylvania's own strong gun control law. Though one of the strongest in the country, Pennsylvania's law is seldom enforced and, in any event, is all too easily circumvented because of illegal trafficking in firearms. The present federal gun control law has proved powerless against this underground market. For this reason, I am skeptical of the potential for success of further attempts both to restrict gun ownership and to control the number of crimes committed with guns.[7]

Ertel's experience—which presumably included his nonenforcement of the law when he was a prosecutor—led him to support a bill that would have amended the 1968 Gun Control Act, which he acknowledged would make it less restrictive. That bill, designed by longtime gun proponents James A. McClure, Idaho Republican, and Harold L. Volkmer, Missouri Democrat, would have eased restrictions on interstate shipment of firearms and made prosecution of violators more difficult. Thus, a Pennsylvanian whose license under the tough state law allowed him to buy unlimited quantities of guns would be given what one newspaper called a green light for gun traffic to any other state in the union.[8]

The election of Ronald Reagan in November 1980 provided the strongest possible support for the gun lobby and those in Congress who sought either to weaken or repeal the 1968 statute. Senator Edward Kennedy's attempt to interest President Reagan in a compromise bill that would ban the importation of the pistol parts used to assemble Saturday night specials proved fruitless. A newspaper columnist who wrote ecstatically about "our indomitable president" ridiculed liberals for their "characteristic maundering" about violence and their inability to understand that the answer was not gun control but a tougher approach to the handling of criminals.[9]

Given the incentive of White House support, the NRA stepped up its public campaign, taking part in a discussion of gun control, hosted by the editor of the *New York Times* Sunday "Week in Review," that brought together Congressman Jonathan Bingham, Lawrence W. Sherman, director of research for the Police Foundation, and James J. Featherstone, general counsel of the National Rifle Association.

Featherstone opened with the standard arguments that better law enforcement, rather than gun control, was needed, and that the worst violence occurred in areas that were "saturated with gun laws." Bingham's response was the oft-repeated argument that "the mishmash of state and local laws" was so inadequate that no one had any difficulty getting hold of a gun, which he called an "out-and-out insane" situation. Sherman compared the effort of individual states to control the weapons trade with the prospect of any one state attempting to control the acid rain that fell within its jurisdiction.[10]

More remarkable was Featherstone's denial that opinion polls had shown most of the public in favor of gun control. The several hundred thousand letters received by the Treasury Department protesting its proposed central registry, he said, overwhelmed the mere 7,000 favorable letters that he charged were solicited by the *New York Times*, *Washington Post* and other newspapers. Further, he said, a poll conducted by an organization called Decision Making Information, which he did not otherwise identify, "came to an opposite conclusion" from polls taken by nationally known agencies referred to by the moderator of the debate. The *Times* editor did not point out that in offerng editorial support for federal gun legislation, the *Times* and *Post* did not indulge in the type of write-your-congressman campaign undertaken repeatedly by the NRA. Sherman observed that the outpouring of mail from those opposed to the Treasury Department's proposals proved only that progun enthusiasts were more inclined to put their views in writing.[11]

The spring of 1981 also saw delegates to the NRA's annual convention vote unanimously for the reelection of Harlon B. Carter as executive vice president of that organization. A few years earlier, Carter had told a congressional committee that he would not favor restrictions on the sale of firearms even to convicted felons, mentally deranged persons and dope addicts, saying this was "a price we pay for freedom."[12]

Boasting in his autobiography that as a federal officer he had supervised the arrest of many thousands of criminals, including murderers, Carter neglected to mention that at the age of 17 he himself had been convicted of murder for shooting to death a 15-year-old Mexican boy. That jury verdict was reversed by a Texas court of appeals, which held that the trial judge had failed to give the jurors "appropriate instruction on the law of self-defense." Asked about the murder in a 1981 interview, Carter denied it, saying the convicted person's first name was Harlan, with an *a*, while his had been Harlon ever since it was inscribed on his birth certificate, and further, that he had been a student at the University of Texas in Austin when the murder was committed in Laredo, some 200 miles away. An investigation of the records revealed the first name on his birth certificate was Harlan with an *a*, which was the same spelling used by his defense attorney in papers submitted at the murder trial. And not until two years later did Carter enroll at the University of Texas when, at that point, he registered as Harlon Carter.[13]

Under Carter's leadership, the NRA undertook in July 1981 a campaign to have the government abolish the Treasury Department's Bureau of Alcohol, Tobacco and Firarms (BATF), the agency responsible for enforcing federal gun-control laws. The principal instrument for putting across the message that BATF inspectors act like "jack-booted fascists" in their treatment of legitimate gun owners was a film entitled *It Can't Happen Here*.[14] One of the principal actors in that film was Democratic Representative John Dingell of Michigan. A member of the board of directors of NRA, Dingell was the originator of the fascist charge against BATF, as he acknowledged in his later testimony before a Senate appropriations subcommittee.

The committee hearing was called to determine whether or not the Appropriations Committee of the Congress should provide funds for the dissolution of BATF.[15] In his presentation Dingell recalled his earlier charge when he said, "If I were to select a jack-booted group of fascists who are perhaps as large a danger of American society as I could pick today, I would pick BATF."[16] He also repeated the account of BATF abuses narrated in the NRA film, going back to 1977 to find the first of three cases in which gun owners were severely mistreated by BATF investigators, who in one case shot and permanently crippled a suspect.

Treasury officials were not asked to comment on the charges made by Dingell, but in a newspaper interview the head of BATF admitted that mistakes had been made but that the film was "grossly misleading" in offering a few selected events as evidence of standard practice. In one of the cases cited in the film, he said, a tape recording of the incident "showed the victims making racial slurs, using profanity and discussing ways guns are sold illegally." An NRA member himself, BATF chief G. R. Dickerson pointed out that all of the horror stories selected by the NRA occurred between 1975 and 1978, prior to his appointment, and took no account of the steps he had taken to prevent a recurrence of such incidents. He also insisted that two-thirds of those actually arrested for violation of firearms laws had prior criminal records involving "narcotics, organized crime and outlaw motorcycle gangs."[17] Dickerson's attempt to bring together government officials, gun manufacturers and NRA representatives to consider how best to prevent thefts of firearms failed when the NRA refused to participate.[18]

Neither the proposal to abolish BATF nor the administration suggestion that its responsibilities and personnel be divided between Customs and the Secret Service was acted upon by Congress. Rather, the contest turned into a tug of war between those who sought to strengthen the 1968 Gun Control Act and those who would weaken or abolish it. A task force appointed by Attorney General William French Smith at the direction of President Reagan was asked to study the problem of violent crime. To the dismay of both Smith and the president, the task force recommended strengthening federal gun controls by requiring gun owners to report thefts to their local police, by withholding delivery of handguns until a check of the buyer's record could be made and by banning the importation of unassembled handgun parts.[19]

In characteristic fashion, President Reagan ignored these recommendations. The only reference to the report for the remainder of 1981 came from White House counsel Edwin Meese, who, in a press interview he shared with the president, cited a task force proposal that "a reasonable standard of bail" be established.[20] Whenever the subject of gun control came up in presidential news conferences, Reagan was as adamant as any other NRA member in insisting that laws already on the books had proved unenforceable and that the only additional laws that would make sense would be those that would increase the penalty for committing a crime with a gun.[21] He held to this position through the entire eight years of his presidency.

Meanwhile, the battle continued at every level—national, state and local. A Virginia-based organization, Gun Owners of America, Inc., circulated a letter addressed to "Dear Fellow Gun Owner" with a questionnaire that purported to be an "Official Congressional District Survey on Violent Crime." Attacking the "new anti-gun recommendations" contained in the report of the Federal Task Force on Violent Crime, the letter promised to send Virginia's two U.S. senators the results of its loaded questionnaire.[22] Pressures of this kind presaged the first sucessful attack on the Gun Control Act of 1968, which came four years later with passage of an amendment to an appropriation bill that removed the record-keeping requirements on sales of .22-caliber rimfire ammunition.[23] The same year (1982), Idaho's Senator James A. McClure introduced a bill whose declared purpose was

to assure that the rights of citizens to keep and bear arms under the second amendment to the United States Constitution; their rights to security against illegal and unreasonable searches and seizures under the fourth amendment; their protection against uncompensated taking of property, double jeopardy, and assurance of due process of law under the fifth amendment; and their rights against unconstitutional exercises of authority under the ninth and tenth amendments are not infringed under enforcement of existing firearm statutes.[24]

Reporting its approval of the bill, the Judiciary Committee declared this protective legislation necessary because of BATF "enforcement practices which are aimed at harassing, burdening, and harming those law-abiding citizens who choose to own and use firearms for legitimate purposes."[25]

The kinds of changes proposed in this bill, which would be fought over for several years, were these:

- Removal of the prohibition against the sale of handguns to out-of-state residents.
- Easing of the ban on mail-order sales where buyer and seller have negotiated the sale "face to face."
- Elimination of the restriction on importing firearms by unlicensed individuals.

- Exemption of sales of ammunition from all record-keeping requirements.
- Permission for private, face-to-face sales of weapons with no record-keeping requirement.
- Requirement of proof of intent to violate the law for conviction.

On the other side were senators, like Massachusetts' Edward M. Kennedy, who believed the 1968 statute needed strengthening, particularly "as it applies to the types of handguns most often used in crime." Changes desired by this group began with a complete ban on handguns of a type "not generally recognized as particularly suitable" for sporting purposes, a 21-day wait before taking possession, and a meticulous record of every sale. Subsequently, demands were made for restrictions on the importation of handgun parts and on the sale or possession of assault weapons and armor-piercing bullets."[26]

If firearms owners did not immediately succeed in getting approval of the McClure bill, it was not for lack of effort. The 1984 campaign mounted by NRA included a new series of "I'm the NRA" ads placed in mass-circulation journals like *Parade* magazine, showing either Hollywood star Charlton Heston holding a rifle, or a beautiful young housewife wielding a very large pistol. A full-page ad in the October 1990 *American Rifleman* featuring a smiling, all-American-type boy reminded NRA members that the organization is "Not Just for Dads." Another part of the drive was conducted by Republican Senator and NRA board member Ted Stevens of Alaska, who sought to have the Post Office strip Handgun Control of its nonprofit mailing status. A third was an "essay" placed as an ad in the Op-Ed page of the *New York Times* by NRA's executive vice president, Harlon B. Carter. In the ad, Carter offered even higher authority than the Constitution in support of his case. Quoting the Declaration of Independence to remind readers that men "are endowed by their Creator with certain unalienable rights," he observed that one of those God-given entitlements was the right to protect one's life and property. And because of its divine origin, Carter said, no government may interfere with an individual's decision to own and use a gun as a means of protection.[27]

Although these efforts did not immediately produce the desired repeal of the Gun Control Act of 1968, by 1986 anticontrol forces had sufficient strength in Congress to bring about a marked revision of that law. Given the unyielding opposition to controls by

President Reagan and Vice President—later President—George Bush, this was not surprising. Still, leaders of the gun-control faction made the most of every opportunity to demonstrate the validity of their point of view. Even in the face of NRA's multi-faceted 1984 campaign, they achieved a measure of success. In October of that year, after a series of court battles with NRA over Morton Grove's 1981 ordinance banning private possession of handguns and other weapons, the Supreme Court of Illinois upheld that law, an action later sustained when the U.S. Supreme Court refused to review the case.[28]

That same month brought to a head a long struggle by police and gun-control advocates to convince Congress of the need for a ban on ther sale of armor-piercing bullets to private individuals. Originally designed for military and police use, the bullets marketed by one manufacturer were advertised as capable of piercing "a concrete block, an automobile engine block, barricade or armor plate." In a 1983 newsletter, the National Coalition to Ban Handguns (NCBH) pointed out that these shells could also penetrate more than four times the thickness of the standard bullet-proof vest used by police officers. NCBH president Michael Beard also attempted to counter the effect of a laudatory address to NRA members by President Reagan, arguing the case for gun control on a number of radio and television talk shows.[29]

Taking no sides, *Congressional Quarterly*'s weekly newsletter noted that although President Reagan had vetoed a drug enforcement bill which contained a "bullet-control" amendment, a new crop of bills to restrict the sale of armor-piercing bullets had "split the pro-gun lobby."[30] The split developed from the difficulty many members of Congress had in publicly defending the right of all individuals to purchase and use in any kind of weapon what had come to be known as "cop-killer" bullets. While at this stage gun-control forces failed to win a total ban on all such ammunition, they did succeed in getting approval of a law that mandated adding five to ten years to the sentence of anyone convicted of a crime of violence who "uses or carries any handgun loaded with armor-piercing ammunition." The law further stipulated that no parole would be permitted during the mandated prison term. Passed by Congress and signed without fanfare by President Reagan, the bill became law on October 12, 1984.[31]

Two years later this measure was further strengthened by a bill banning completely the production and importation of all armor-piercing bullets.[32] Passed in the Senate by a vote of 97 to 1 and in the House by 400 to 21, H.R. 3132 was signed by President Reagan in a ceremony in which he boasted of having for six and one-half years done "everything possible to protect the lives and safety of the dedicated men and women who constitute our first line of defense against the forces of lawlessness." Ironically, most of the fourteen police organizations he then cited as supporting this legislation had long urged the more stringent gun controls that Reagan had persistently opposed.[33]

That same year, anticontrol forces won a far more important victory with passage of the Firearms Owners' Protection Act.[34] President Reagan's support of this law, which eliminated many of the restrictions in the 1968 Gun Control Act, led a reporter to ask why, "in light of your own experience, in light of the opposition of various police groups as well as Mrs. Brady to this legislation . . . why do you support virtually no limits on gun control at this point?" Denying that it was "a no limit thing," Reagan repeated the standard argument that cities with the tightest controls had the highest crime rates, and "as long as there are guns, the individual that wants a gun for a crime is going to have one and going to get it." The reporter did not challenge Reagan's implied assumption that as controls are tightened the crime rate goes up. His further fictional account of British law and tradition, cited earlier, ended questions on that subject.[35]

Purporting to build on the 1968 Gun Control Act's intention not "to discourage or eliminate the private ownership or use of firearms by law-abiding citizens for lawful purposes," the new law did, in fact, eliminate many of the restrictions of the earlier act. Control over retail sales of ammunition—except for armor-piercing bullets—was lifted; the Secretary of the Treasury's power to establish regulations was curtailed; conviction of a crime would depend upon the effectiveness of local legislation, as it would "be determined in accordance with the law of the jurisdiction in which the proceedings were held"; application of the law was limited to manufacturers and dealers who make firearms trade their "principal objective of livelihood and profit," thus eliminating part-time dealers and collectors, the latter being deliberately excluded from the law enforcement provisions; the ban on interstate transfer of handguns acquired "by bequest or intestate succession" was lifted; interstate sale of rifles and shotguns was not prohibited if legal in both the buyer's and seller's states and arranged by the transferee meeting "in person" with the transferor; prosecution was made more difficult by the requirement that violations must be proven to have been made "willfully"; warrants obtained for search in cases of suspected violations could be served only "during business hours," and nonwarranted inspections of records were limited to "not more than once during any twelve-month period."[36]

Even the 1934 National Firearms Act was modified to reduce the ban on machine gun parts to those intended "solely and exclusively" for use in converting a weapon into a machine gun. And, finally, to preclude interference with the new federal law by a less permissive state or municipality, a blanket statement declared:

Any person not prohibited by this chapter from transporting, shipping, or receiving a firearm should be entitled to transport an unloaded, not readily accessible firearm in interstate commerce notwithstanding any provision of any legislation enacted, or any rule or regulation prescribed by any state or political subdivision thereof.[37]

Not content with the support given gun owners by the nation's highest legislative and executive authorities, the Citizens Committee for the Right to Keep and Bear Arms petitioned the Vatican to designate Saint Gabriel Possenti patron saint of handgun owners. Basing this request on a tale that Saint Gabriel's own order declared to be "without foundation," Citizens Committee lobbyist John M. Snyder called the saint "sort of a holy John Wayne" for his purported feat of saving a nineteenth-century Italian village from bandits by threatening them with a pair of pistols.[38] The petition was renewed four years later and, as before, was ignored by the Vatican.[39]

Because of the attempted assassination of President Reagan by pistol-wielding John Hinckley, the focus of attention centered on handguns whenever the subject came up in a Reagan speech or press conference. And throughout the 1988 campaign for the election of George Bush, Reagan's references to this subject repeated the same theme over and over, that "our side" believes that "law-abiding people who want to protect their home and family have a constitutional right to own guns." Democratic opponents he consistently referred to as "the liberals," and his statement that "the liberals favor gun control" was an accusation that they were indifferent to the safety and welfare of the average American.[40]

By the close of the Reagan administration, the increasing use of assault-type weapons in gang wars and drug wars and by individuals seeking either vengeance, profit or an outlet for expressing their rage against society brought increasing attention to the danger posed by the ready availability of these weapons. In one of President Bush's earliest exchanges with reporters, questions turned to the subject of assault rifles. Asked about his attitude toward the "rampant" use of these guns, the president reminded his questioner that there were already laws outlawing the importation of fully automatic AK-47s. Pressed to take a similar stand on semiautomatic weapons, one of which had been used in a schoolyard massacre of children in Stockton, California, Bush refused to do so. Taking the NRA tack of associating these weapons with hunting, Bush said, "I'm not about to suggest that a semi-automatic hunting rifle be banned." No reporter at this session asked any of the questions that normally flow from a reporter's who-what-when-where-why inquiry, such as whether the president ever owned, ever used or ever saw anyone else use a semiautomatic rifle of the "assault" type for hunting, or if he knew how easily semiautomatics could be converted to fully automatic weapons capable of firing anywhere from 120 to 500 bullets in 60 seconds, or if he had never been influenced by his wife Barbara's abhorrence of guns or by her statement that "for thirty-five years I have been for gun control," and her comment—made only two weeks after he had assumed the presidency—that AK-47s should be made illegal, "absolutely."[41]

Part of the answer to the first of these unasked questions came later in the year, when Bush volunteered the information that when he was a congressman he took his hunting "arsenal" to the District of Columbia police headquarters to be registered. The arsenal, he said, consisted of "a .22 and .410," neither of which could be classified as an assault weapon.[42] Nevertheless, Bush had his guns registered as the local law required, without using the occasion to protest the requirement as an invasion of his constitutional rights. Nor did he echo his wife's earlier remark, "I just don't think it's any big deal to register a gun."[43] His contrary stand, refusing to consider a ban on semiautomatic weapons, was voiced less than two weeks after Barbara had expressed an opposing view. Although the First Lady never altered her opinion on this subject, once it became a public issue, out of loyalty to her husband she refused to make any further comment on gun control.

Bills to outlaw private possession of assault weapons had been introduced in Congress and in some state legislatures during the Reagan years, but few survived beyond the committee stage. The first breakthrough occurred not in the nation's capital but in Reagan's home state of California. On January 16, 1989, Patrick Purdy sprayed a Stockton schoolyard with bullets from a semi-automatic AKM-47 rifle designed by the Chinese for military use. Thirty of the children in the yard were shot and five were killed. Within two months the cities of Stockton, Palo Alto and Los Angeles had enacted laws banning military-style assault rifles. And on May 24 California's governor signed a bill that declared:

The Legislature hereby finds ... that the proliferation and use of assault weapons pose a serious threat to the health, safety, and security of all citizens of this state. The Legislature has restricted the assault weapons ... based upon finding that each firearm has such a high rate of fire and capacity for firepower that its function as a legitimate sports or recreational firearm is substantially out-weighed by the danger that it can be used to kill and injure human beings.[44]

The law not only identified 23 varieties of rifles, 7 pistols, and 2 shotguns as assault weapons, it also authorized the state's Superior Court to extend the ban, after a hearing to consider the evidence, to any weapon found to be identical to those listed "except for slight modifications or enhancements."[45]

The California statute was immediately challenged in the courts by the NRA on two grounds: that it violated the Second Amendment right to bear arms and that it outlawed one of the weapons used in carrying out the federal law governing a civilian marksmanship program. After three years of litigation, a federal court of appeals rejected both arguments, pointing out that the Supreme Court's 1876 decision that the Second Amendment was binding only on Congress had never been overturned, and that eliminating one of the weapons used in the marksmanship competition had no significant effect on the overall program.[46]

At the federal level, the perennial cluster of handgun bills was accompanied by several dealing with control of assault weapons. Those deemed most effecitve—and most threatening to the NRA— were identified in *American Hunter* as Senate bills S. 747 and S. 386, introduced by Dennis DeConcini and Howard M. Metzenbaum, respectively, and House bills H.R. 1154 and H.R. 1190, authored by

Sam Gibbons of Florida and Fortney H. (Pete) Stark, whose California residence in Alameda County was only a short distance from Stockton.[47] When a House committee hearing was held to consider a group of these bills, the subject was considered serious enough to warrant public hearings, with coverage by radio, television, newspaper and magazine reporters. During two days of hearings in April 1989, the committee considered a number of firearms bills, including several dealing with handgun control. But as the chairman acknowledged in his lengthy introduction,

the gun issue on which the attention of the Nation, from the President on down, has been riveted in recent weeks and months is the issue which has come to be known as the assault weapons problem. These are weapons which, in many cases, were developed to be used by military forces to defend citizens against foreign enemies in combat. The military aura which surrounds them, summed up in one word, "Rambo," seems to appeal to drug traffickers and other violent offenders. It also seems to appeal to a wide range of mentally deranged individuals who, with increasing frequency, arm themselves with one or more of these weapons and in one sickening outburst of indiscriminate and massive firepower acquire for themselves an infamous spot in American history. . . .

These assault weapons are designed for one purpose: to kill as many human beings as possible as quickly as possible. Hunters do not favor them, as their range is relatively short, and their firepower too destructive. State gaming laws do not permit their use, nor are they particularly suitable for target shooting, since the targets these weapons tend to be zeroed in on are full-sized human silhouettes. This may be appropriate for military or police training, but I find little compelling need to recognize this sort of shooting as a legitimate sporting purpose. The casual gun owner who keeps a firearm for the protection of life and family has no need for a weapon used by soldiers and commandos.[48]

The pros and cons of this issue, discussed for hours in the hearings, were effectively condensed in the documents submitted by both control and anticontrol advocates. The NRA offered an abstract of "Facts on So-Called Assault Weapons" that included these statements:

Technically, the correct definition of an assault rifle is a selective-fire military rifle. As such, they are fully-automatic firearms for the purposes of federal law. The AKM-47 (actually a Model 565, a copy of the AKM-47) used by Patrick Purdy in his heinous crime in Stockton, California, on

January 17th is a semi-automatic rifle functionally identical to millions of semi-automatic rifles owned by hunters and sportsmen in the United States for nearly a century. It was not converted to fully-automatic fire, nor is it "readily convertible." That semiautomatic rifle is no more "powerful" or more "rapid-fire" than any other semi-automatic hunting and target rifle owned by millions of Americans. Purdy's lack of a felony record meant he could and did comply with and pass the 15-day waiting period and police background check required under California law to purchase five pistols. It was the criminal justice system that failed those schoolchildren in the tragic incident in Stockton.[49]

Procontrol organizations offered evidence that

assault weapons legislation was being considered in 16 states, was pending in 14 and had been defeated in only 2. BATF had announced on April 5, 1989, the temporary suspension of 40 different types of semiautomatic firearms, including the AK-47. Many of these weapons are listed in the authoritative military source book, *Jane's Infantry Weapons.*

In the two years prior to President Bush's ban on imports of assault rifles, imports of the AK-47 increased 1,000 percent.[50]

The White House contribution to this subject was Press Secretary Marlin Fitzwater's April 5 announcement that "in an effort to ensure that existing laws are being enforced to the fullest extent possible, he [the president] ordered a review of the suitability of these [imported] weapons for sporting purposes." That review had been ordered on March 14, the day the "temporary suspension" of imports was established. The only result announced on April 5 was an expansion of the list of banned weapons. The twofold purpose of the expansion was explained this way:

First, those importers whose permits were suspended on March 14 will not suffer a loss of market to importers of similar weapons during the review period. Second, this action will preclude flooding the market with firearms which might later be found unsuitable for sporting purposes.[51]

This explanation failed to impress supporters of assault-weapons legislation, who were convinced that American manufacturers could flood the market without any help from foreign gun makers. Thus, efforts to push controls continued. In the Senate, Joseph R. Biden of Delaware introduced a bill "to establish constitutional procedures for imposition of the sentence of death, and for other purposes." One of the other purposes was an "Anti-drug, Assault Weapons Limitation Act." Because this latter section was buried behind forty-five pages devoted to the death penalty, habeas corpus reform and the exclusionary rule, the NRA saw the bill as a deceitful maneuver to use capital punishment, which it approved, as camouflage for slipping a gun control measure through Congress. Notwithstanding Biden's previous support of NRA policies, including voting against a bill mandating a 7-day wait for handgun purchasers, he was immediately added to the NRA list of legislators to be bombarded with opposition letters. Even as it took comfort in the fact that none of the 1989 bills were approved, thanks to "victories wrought solely by NRA members," that organization pressed its campaign in 1990 with the charge that Senator Biden "would have Americans keep good records or go to jail."[52]

For gun control advocates, 1990 was as unproductive as 1989. True, New Jersey followed California's lead in banning private purchase of semiautomatic assault weapons, but similar legislation continued to lag in the second session of the 101st Congress. A key test had come with a subcommittee vote on S. 747 and S. 386. The vote to report both bills to the full Judiciary Committee "without recommendation" passed by a narrow margin, 7 Democrats in favor, 5 Republicans and 1 Democrat opposed, and 1 Republican not voting.[53] To counter endorsements of the bills by groups like the New York Academy of Medicine, Vermont State Association of Chiefs of Police and other state and international police officials cited earlier, NRA had culled the names of 225 police officers from its files and organized them into a "march on the Capital." Representative Philip M. Crane of Illinois provided supporting evidence by putting into the *Congressional Record* the claim that "over 100,000 police officers say 'no' to proposals that restrict our right to possess certain firearms." This undocumented assertion Crane found in an advertisement in the September 10, 1990, issue of *Roll Call* which, as the reader discovered at the very end of the Crane's 5-minute speech, was paid for by the American Shooting Sports Coalition.[54]

President Bush had also come under attack by a member of NRA for his ban on imports of semiautomatic assault rifles, and had to be defended by the organization's executive vice president in an article that pointed out that the president's actions couldn't compare to "even a preamble to a Dukakis package."[55] That same issue of the NRA's official journal updated the tally of bills to ban semiautomatic weapons, reporting that such measures had been introduced in twenty-four states, that they had been defeated in fifteen and had an uncertain future in all the rest except California, which had succeeded in enacting such a law.[56]

As the heat continued to build in 1990, Robert MacNeil and James Lehrer, for the second time in twelve months, took up the question of assault weapons. Invited as participants were pro-control Senator Metzenbaum, anticontrol Senator Hatch, shooting victim James Brady, and NRA spokesman Wayne LaPierre. On both sides the arguments remained the same as before, but moderator Roger Mudd prefaced the discussion with statistics on gun ownership that indicated that some 70 million Americans own guns and the number of weapons sold at retail was adding 7.5 million to the total each year. Between 60 and 70 percent of those questioned were reported as owning single-shot weapons, 25 percent having semiautomatics.[57]

The month following MacNeil/Lehrer's April program saw several notable events. New Jersey banned the private purchase of assault weapons, and a publication entitled *Full Auto, Volume One, AR-15 Modification Manual* offered mail-order customers complete information on how to make an "illegal machine gun" out of a legally purchased semiautomatic rifle.[58] May in Helotes, Texas, was the occasion for the Third Annual Hill Country Machine Gun Shoot, open to shooters of all ages, as indicated by the news photo of a grim looking 10-year-old boy firing an M-16 with the aid of an adult participant.[59] In that month's NRA journal, president Joe Foss urged all members to combat the "anti–law-enforcement lies" against his organization by recruiting new members from their local police departments.[60] And in June the magazine featured a pair of articles purporting to destroy the "skewed interpretation of the Second Amendment" authored earlier by former Chief Justice of the U.S. Supreme Court, Warren E. Berger.[61]

Senator Robert Byrd had a few remarks about lies from the other side. Responding to a circular letter distributed by the NRA, Byrd characterized as "patently false" the letter's charge that "the De-Concini gun ban bill survived by one vote and [West Virginia Senators] Jay Rockefeller and Robert Byrd betrayed every honest gun owner in West Virginia by voting for it." Quoting another NRA statement that "it is only a question of time before every gun you own is taken away because some politician wants to pretend he is fighting crime," Byrd reminded his Senate colleagues that, as a gun owner himself, he knew assault guns were not needed for either hunting or personal protection, that they are the weapons of "mass murderers, cop killers, kid killers, and drug dealers." Voicing the suspicion that the NRA had probably sent a letter like the one he quoted to the constituents of every senator who had voted to keep the DeConcini measure in the broad anticrime bill, he said the effect of that campaign had been to confuse legitimate gun owners. They were being led to believe, he said, that supporters of the assault-weapon ban want to deny law-abiding citizens the right to own the kinds of rifles, shotguns and pistols normally used for hunting and self-protection. He assured the "50,000 upstanding NRA members in West Virginia" that he would always defend their right to keep hunting and sporting guns and those needed to protect their families, and labelled any suggestion to the contrary as false and misleading propaganda.[62]

New York's Senator Daniel Patrick Moynihan was even more explicit in his charge that the NRA cares nothing about any of the nation's problems except "guns, guns and more guns." In a letter to his constituents, he distinguished between "the many people who are members of the National Rifle Association and the small number of professional lobbyists who run the political and propaganda operations of the NRA." The latter he scorned as "a notorious crowd" who, "like all good lobbyists ... know that there's one sure-fire way to bring waverers in the Senate and the House back into line." The method they planned to use in the 1990 congressional elections, he wrote, would be this: "You pick out a Senator or Member of Congress who faces a close election ... and you commit whatever resources are necessary to remove that person from office. This November, that is precisely what the leaders of the NRA plan to do."[63] The NRA was equally frank in bearing out Moynihan's forecast. Early fall issues of its official journal listed and rated not only candidates for the U.S. Senate and House but for state legislatures and governorships. The ratings, from A+ for those who have "gone the extra mile" in support of NRA policies to F and ? for active or suspected opponents of those policies, were offered as a guide to voters interested in electing "pro-gun/pro-sportsmen candidates."[64]

Although it did not succeed in removing its major enemies from public office, the NRA could justifiably boast at the close of the year, "The 101st Congress Has Ended ... And Victory Is Ours!" As explained in a review of "nearly 70 anti-gun proposals" put before Congress during the 1989–1990 term, not one survived. Particularly satisfying, the article said, were the ultimate defeat of the ban on semiautomatic weapons, described by the NRA reporter as "the main goal of the NRA Institute," and the "derailing of the Brady Bill."[65]

Neither side relaxed its efforts during the 102nd Congress. Early in the first 1991 session, a striking defection from NRA ranks occurred when Ronald Reagan wrote an op-ed article for the *New York Times* entitled "Why I'm for the Brady Bill." Noting that March 30 would be the tenth anniversary of the attempt on his life, he reminded *Times* readers that his press secretary, James A. Brady, was still living in pain from the bullet that had passed through his brain. Then, in a complete reversal of the position he had steadfastly maintained throughout the eight years of his presidency, he said, "This nightmare might never have happened if legislation that is before Congress now—the Brady Bill—had been law back in 1981." The balance of his article, which refuted his earlier stand and echoed the very arguments Jim and Sarah Brady had been making for years, included these statements:

Named for Jim Brady, this legislation would establish a national seven-day waiting period before a handgun purchaser could take delivery. It would allow local law enforcement officials to do background checks for criminal records or known histories of mental disturbances. Those with such records would be prohibited from buying the handguns. . . . Based upon the evidence in states that already have handgun purchase waiting periods, this bill—on a nationwide scale—can't help but stop thousands of illegal handgun purchases.

Critics claim that "waiting period" legislation in the states that have it doesn't work, that criminals just go to nearby states that lack such laws to buy their weapons. True enough, and all the more reason to have a Federal law that fills the gaps. . . .

Even with the current gaps among states, those that have waiting periods report some success. California, which has a 15-day waiting period that I supported and signed into law while Governor, stopped nearly 1,800 prohibited handgun sales in 1989.[66]

This statement made front-page news, along with a report that Reagan had visited with President Bush to suggest that he end his opposition to the Brady bill. Promising only to "reconsider" the matter, Bush appeared to modify his stand two months later when, in answer to a reporter's question, he said, "we will consider it if it is attached to the comprehensive crime bill."[67] However, through the remainder of 1991 and the first four months of 1992, his comments on this subject—made on twenty occasions—stressed the need for Congress to pass his Comprehensive Violent Crime Control Bill. The principal elements in this proposal were: (1) the death penalty "for drug kingpins and for certain heinous acts such as terrorist murders of American nationals abroad, killing of hostages, and murder for hire"; (2) restricted use of habeas corpus to limit "the ability of Federal and State prisoners to file repetitive habeas corpus petitions"; (3) modification of the exclusion rule to permit "the use of evidence that has been seized by Federal or State law enforcement officials acting in 'good faith'"; and (4) an increase in firearms offenses and penalties.[68]

Repeatedly, Bush referred to his "challenge" to Congress "to act within 100 days" on his crime bill.[69] At one point he misrepresented the position of those who objected to some aspects of his proposal when he explained their differences this way:

You see, there's two schools of thought: one, we need to worry a little more about the criminals and their rights and soften the criminal anti-crime legislation, hoping that you can rehabilitate; and there's another school of thought, which is mine, and that is that we need to be tougher on crime.[70]

On November 24, a joint House-Senate conference committee reached agreement on a bill that included the Brady waiting period and added funding for drug treatment for federal prisoners and for additional officers to aid local law enforcement. It also included all of the death sentence provisions in the Bush bill, as well as the mandatory prison terms he recommended for crimes committed with guns. Otherwise, the major difference between the agreed-upon measure and the bill supported by President Bush was the absence of the Bush provision that would permit a federal court to refuse a habeas corpus hearing requested by a prisoner who the judge decided had been given a fair hearing in state courts.[71]

President Bush called the result "so weak and so soft on criminals that I'll have to veto it if it reaches my desk."[72] This threat encouraged Republicans in the Senate to filibuster the compromise measure, both before and after it had been passed by the House. Three days after the conference committee completed its work, an attempt to limit debate in the Senate was defeated when only 49 of the 60 votes required supported the cloture motion. The following March 19 a second test brought the vote to 54–43 in favor of cloture, still 6 short of the needed three-fifths. For all practical purposes this ended the 102nd Congress's effort to pass an anticrime bill.[73]

A last-ditch effort in support of control legislation by Handgun Control proved fruitless, although in its circular letter, signed by James S. Brady, it quoted with devastating effect this portion of a letter circulated by progun lobbyist Neal Knox: "Not only did we knock every gun section out of the House crime bill, in the teeth of the nation's worst mass-shooting, we reversed the perception that the gun lobby is a paper tiger." The Brady letter mistakenly associated Knox with the National Rifle Association, but it made its point by identifying him as a man "who's actually happy that the same vile instrument of death used to kill and injure 45 innocent people in the Killeen, Texas, massacre will still be available for purchase over the counter in gun stores."[74]

For President Bush, his 1988–1992 term failed to produce an anticrime law that would not only increase the penalties for criminal acts but provide police and the courts with broader powers for warrantless searches and for rejecting habeas corpus petitions from the state to federal courts. For gun-control advocates, the Bush years were also a period of failure, despite widespread public support for strict control of both handguns and assault weapons. Only the gun lobby could claim victory for having been instrumental in preventing enactment of any significant gun legislation.

The first glimmer of hope for control advocates came with the defeat of George Bush in his run for reelection and the election of Bill Clinton as president. Although not a significant factor in an election dominated by concerns about jobs and a lagging economy, gun control was important enough to warrant a paragraph in each candidate's platform. Bush's pledge stated:

Republicans defend the constitutional right to keep and bear arms. We call for stiff mandatory sentences for those who use firearms in a crime. We note that those who seek to disarm citizens in their homes are the same liberals who tried to disarm our Nation during the Cold War and are today seeking to cut our national defense below safe levels. We applaud congressional Republicans for overturning the District of Columbia's law blaming firearm manufacturers for street crime.[75]

The corresponding section of the Democratic platform, labelled "Community Policy," also condemned street violence and promised support not only for the Brady bill but for "controls to ban the possession, sale, importation and manufacture of the most deadly assault weapons." To defend against the charge that control advocates are soft on criminals and secretly intend to make all gun ownership illegal, this assurance was added:

We do not support efforts to restrict weapons used for legitimate hunting and sporting purposes. We will work for swift and certain punishment of all people who violate the country's gun laws and for stronger sentences for criminals who use guns. We will also seek to shut down the black market for guns and impose severe penalties on people who sell guns to children.[76]

During the campaign, the media devoted more attention to the subject of gun control than the candidates did, thanks to the continuing widespread sale and use of guns in criminal activity. Editorially, the New York Times supported a bill, proposed in both the District of Columbia and New York City, that would apply product liability laws to arms manufacturers in the same way as to other campanies whose products caused harm to members of the general public.[77] A week later the wife of James Brady attempted to address a University of Nevada audience on the merits of the Brady bill but was shouted down by anti-gun-control activists who could not be restrained by university authorities.[78]

Reports of increasing violence and rising sales of home security systems led to a five-part series of articles in the New York Times entitled "200 Million Guns," the number estimated to be in private possession in the United States in March 1992. Surveying the gun scene, reporters found what a major arms retailer called a "gun culture" in which the expanding market for weapons was accounted for largely by popular reaction to daily reports of violence throughout the nation, in other words, people seeking a means of self-protection. The manufacturers' response to this demand was to produce greater quantities of increasingly sophisticated weapons for home use. The maker of the Tec-9 semiautomatic pistol, for example, advertised this item as a "fun gun," admirably suited to personal protection as well as target shooting. A Chicago police superintendent declared the Tec-9 too dangerous even for police use, because its thirty-two-round magazine "is designed to spray whole groups of people."[79] Nevertheless, advertisements continued to offer not only weapons but every conceivable type of service, from kits showing how to convert a Chinese semiautomatic assault rifle to fully automatic, to instructions for making a bazooka or a hand grenade.[80]

The frantic rush of householders to arm themselves against threats of harm had no effect on public attitudes toward gun control. A *New York Times*/CBS poll, conducted in late spring, revealed that 86 percent of the general population still favored a waiting period for handgun sales, with 82 percent of gun owners agreeing with this judgment. Almost as many (79 percent of all respondents and 76 percent of gun owners) favored a ban on semiautomatic military-style assault rifles.[81] About the same time, the Missouri legislature considered (but rejected) a bill that would allow private citizens to carry concealed weapons, while Connecticut lawmakers agonized over (but did not alter) that state's partial ownership of the Colt Manufacturing Company, a major producer of handguns and assault rifles.[82]

Although the candidates volunteered little on the subject of gun control, the media sought out and reported whatever opinions they had expressed. As early as April 5, a *New York Times* summary of candidate positions on a variety of issues noted that as governor of Arkansas Clinton had approved a law, supported by the NRA, making harassment of hunters a crime, but he had vetoed an NRA-sponsored bill to prevent local jurisdictions from establishing firearm regulations. How Bush would have reacted to these two situations was not reported, but his belief that local restrictions on gun ownership do not keep weapons out of the hands of criminals was well known.

As election day drew closer, Clinton included in his speech in Chicago a charge that Bush had killed the crime bill he had urged upon Congress "because he didn't want to stand up to the NRA and be for the Brady bill." Enlarging on this subject during the second televised debate with Bush and Perot, held October 15, he declared that while he supported the right to keep and bear arms, "we have to have some way of checking handguns before they're sold." More than this, Clinton said, "we should have restrictions on assault weapons whose only purpose is to kill." Bush's response to the question on gun control focused on those elements of the crime bill he had supported: limited use of habeas corpus, greater freedom for police in making arrests and securing evidence, and a stronger death penalty. He made no direct reference to the Brady bill, stating only that he was "not for national registration of arms" or for "eliminating all kinds of weapons."[83] A final evaluation of Clinton's collected remarks on gun control interpreted them to indicate that he was "receptive to still stronger reform, like universal gun registration and licensing."[84]

Once in office, President Clinton acted promptly to make good on his campaign promise to see the Brady bill enacted into law. On seven occasions during his first eight months in the White House, he repeated to the media, to student groups and to private organizations his desire to have the Brady bill passed. "If Congress will pass it, I will sign it," he told reporters during a discussion of his proposed anticrime legislation. In the same exchange he announced that he was issuing two directives to the secretary of the treasury, one "ordering that the rules governing gun dealers be reviewed to make sure that only legitimate gun dealers are in the business of selling guns," the other "ordering the Treasury Department to take the necessary action to suspend the importation of foreign-made assault pistols, which have become the weapons of choice for many gangs and drug dealers."[85]

The final test of the Brady bill came in November 1993. By a vote of 238 to 189 the House approved a 5-day waiting period for purchasers of handguns, after bowing to NRA pressure to stipulate that the law would expire after five years, which would give the states time to computerize their criminal records for instant checking on gun purchasers. Even with this compromise, Senate Republicans led by Bob Dole resisted passage of the bill until the day before Thanksgiving, when Congress was to conclude its work for the year. The final voice vote approving the bill occurred when only three senators were left on the floor, the remainder having taken off for home earlier in the week.[86]

One month later, a different kind of campaign opened in New York City when, as part of the Christmas celebration, a Dominican rug dealer named Fernando Mateo purchased $5,000 worth of Toys-R-Us gift certificates and offered a $100 certificate to every person who would turn in a gun to the local police station. Others joined the crusade, Foot Locker donating $25,000 worth of certificates, and the NAACP and two police unions adding $10,000 to the fund. Unlike the limited returns brought by the city's already existing amnesty offer of $75 in cash for every gun turned in, with no penalty and no questions asked, the toys-for-guns program reaped a harvest of 317 guns the first week and more than 1,100 two weeks later. Its initial success brought additional donations and encouraged local business leaders to form a committee to expand and extend the program.[87]

New York's official buy-back scheme was not new. Two years earlier, St. Louis had been so successful in buying up privately owned weapons that the offer of $50 for a handgun and $25 for a rifle had brought in 7,547 guns in a single month and so taxed the police department's budget that the plan had to be abandoned. A 1994 Guns for Goods program in Connecticut suffered a similar fate, bankrupting the $100,000 fund contributed by commercial donors in the short space of five days, when 4,200 guns were turned in. In both cases, the returns showed clearly that although these efforts reduced the number of guns that otherwise might have caused deaths or injuries through misuse, accident or uncontrollable impulse, few if any of the owners who turned in their weapons were criminals.[88]

It was the novelty of New York's toys-for-guns idea that appealed to both police and fear-driven residents of gun-plagued cities everywhere. In Florida the *Miami Herald* featured the story on its front page and predicted that similar programs "may spread around the nation." In fact, the spread occurred so rapidly that before the year 1994 was a week old, Dallas was offering to take guns in exchange for Cowboy tickets, Los Angeles had started a goods-for-guns program, and commercial sponsors had chimed in with offers of mattresses for guns, gas for guns and a variety of groceries for guns. Featured on the "MacNeil/Lehrer NewsHour," the impact of the gun-swapping strategy was assessed by a panel that included two police chiefs, a law professor, an educator and a public official. The Charleston, South Carolina, police chief could see no effect on the level of crime, as the people turning in guns were not criminals. Acknowledging this as well as the fact that the number of weapons surrendered would amount to only a drop in the bucket, other speakers saw every gun taken out of circulation as elimination of a potentially lethal hazard. More important was the view that the popularity of the program was evidence of a nationwide turn away from the gun-obsessed violence afflicting American society. Coincidentally, two days before Christmas, Wal-Mart, the country's largest retail chain, announced that on February 1, 1994, it would discontinue the sale of handguns, keeping only a stock of rifles and shotguns for legitimate hunters.[89]

December 1993 also produced a new push for a major expansion of federal controls when Handgun Control issued a "Proposed Comprehensive Bill" whose recommended provisions were capsuled on the cover of an eight-page release in this fashion:

Requires a license to buy a handgun; mandates fingerprint checks and safety training for license applicants; includes a permanent 7-day cooling-off period; and requires the registration of handgun transfers.

Prohibits gun possession by those convicted of violent misdemeanors, including spousal abuse and child abuse; and requires a special license for the possession of a gun arsenal (20 guns or 1000 rounds of ammunition).

Requires gun dealers to pay an annual license fee of $1000; prohibits the sale of more than one handgun a month to any individual; mandates a federal license for ammunition dealers; requires background checks for gun store employees; bans firearms sales at gun shows; and creates a private cause of action for gun law violations.

Bans semiautomatic assault weapons, Saturday Night Special handguns, and non-sporting ammunition; regulates gun safety; and increases the surtax on handguns and handgun ammunition.[90]

Counterattacks by progun organizations ranged from charges that this was intended to extend the ban on assault weapons contained in the omnibus crime bill sponsored by Senator Dianne Feinstein of California, to warnings of a "conspiracy to deprive honest Americans of liberty." This last counterstroke appeared to be a newspaper columnist's reaction to Senate bill 1882, introduced by Howard Metzenbaum, which incorporated many of the proposals contained in the Handgun Control release of the previous December 8. Labelling Senator Metzenbaum and his cosponsor in the House, Representative Charles Schumer, "two of the most obnoxious and intellectually dishonest members of Congress," the columnist went on to describe the pending legislation as "part of a devious scheme hatched in the bowels of Handgun Control Inc."[91] In support of this charge, the writer quoted from what he claimed was a Handgun Control memorandum dated January 6, 1994, and stamped "Confidential Information for use by Lobbyists and Senior Officials ONLY!"

An inquiry to Handgun Control produced a response from the president of that organization, who stated that the memorandum referred to by the newspaper columnist was "a hoax." The following evidence was offered to support this contention:

Handgun Control unveiled its comprehensive legislative agenda (copy attached) at a press conference on December 8, 1993, at the National Press Club in Washington. I'm sure you would agree that this is hardly the best way to keep our plans under wraps. Additionally, the distribution list of the bogus document includes the name "N. T. Shields.". . . Pete Shields, a founder of Handgun Control, passed away in January 1993, almost a year before this memo is alleged to have been written. Other inaccuracies include a reference to January being critical to the importance of Senator Feinstein's proposed ban on assault weapons. This amendment had already passed as part of the Senate's omnibus crime bill in November of last year. Additionally, the document Charley Reese refers to, includes such ridiculous proposals as banning the wearing of combat boots and outlawing hunting parties of four or more individuals.[92]

The seriousness of the implication of overt fraud led this writer to inquire of the columnist's editor as to the source and authenticity of the document cited by the columnist. The ensuing correspondence between this writer, columnist Charley Reese and Handgun Control, Inc. (HCI) president Richard M. Aborn illustrates the difficulty an independent investigator faces in attempting to reduce to verifiable facts the assertions and counterassertions of opponents debating a highly emotional issue.

An answer to the inquiry addressed to the newspaper editor came from columnist Charley Reese, who enclosed with his letter an eight-page document identified as the "corrected version of 'Atatchment 1' [sic] of the HCI memo."[93] In his covering letter, Reese pointed out, correctly, that the enclosure contained none of the references to Shields, Senator Feinstein and combat boots mentioned in Aborn's letter. But as the document was only an attachment to a purported HCI letter, it left a question as to the contents of the letter itself. Further, the attachment was not a photocopy of the original document, but a "corrected transcript" made by an individual whose source of information was not revealed.

To keep the playing field even, copies of Reese's letter and the first page of Attachment 1 were forwarded to Aborn at Handgun Control, together with a request for a copy of the memorandum in which Aborn had found the inaccuracies cited in his earlier letter. Simultaneously, a further inquiry was sent to Reese asking for a copy of the memorandum accompanying Attachment 1, and more precise identification of the transcribers of the attachment. As of this writing, two months later, only one response had been received.

The absence of any communication from Reese may be explained in part by the reluctance every news reporter has for identifying his sources. However, the question as to why only Attachment 1 of the purported HCI memo was supplied, and not the memo itself, did not call for information regarding the source of this material.

Aborn's response to the follow-up questions included a copy of the purported memorandum and Attachment 1. As Aborn had claimed, the memo did include references to Pete Shields, to Senator Feinstein, to a ban on wearing military combat gear and to outlawing hunting parties of more than four people. Aborn's Attachment 1 was identical to Reese's except for three concluding pages headed "A Quick Guide to Arguing with the Gun Zealots," which was not included in the Reese copy.

Given the confirmation supplied by Aborn and the absence of any explanation from Reese as to why he used only the attachment and not the memorandum itself, it would appear that the reporter relied on a document which was, as HCI insisted, a hoax. If this was the case, it suggests a degree of panic in some quarters of the progun community.

Meanwhile, the seriousness of the Clinton administration's intentions became evident when Vice President Gore circulated a letter in April 1994 urging support for the president's most vital legislative proposals, which he said were "to reform our health care system, make our streets safe, change our welfare system, and reduce gun violence in our nation." Simultaneously, the press reported that President Clinton had again pressed Congress to pass his crime control measures, including a bill that would ban the sale of a variety of assault weapons to private individuals.[94]

Until the very last minute, every informal poll and every press report indicated that the assault-weapons bill, which the Senate had passed the previous session, would go down to defeat in the House. The prediction—even by White House aides—was that the bill needed 15 more votes than its supporters could muster. Only a last 24-hour marathon of telephone calls from the president to House members brought in the necessary votes. Even Clinton admitted, after the final tally revealed a favorable vote of 216 to 214, that he "didn't expect to win."[95]

This touch-and-go experience was repeated when the assault-weapons ban was included in the broader crime bill debated in the summer of 1994. Approved by the House after the total cost of additional police, new prisons and crime-prevention programs had been reduced from $33 billion to $30.2 billion, the bill passed the Senate only with the support of six Republicans, which gave the administration the 61 votes needed to turn back a Republican point-of-order challenge that would have blocked passage of the bill. And although Senator Dole kept insisting that the major flaw to which opponents of the bill objected was the unnecessary expense of the crime-prevention measures, Republican Whip Alan Simpson stated flatly on the August 25 "MacNeil/Lehrer News-Hour" that a vote on cloture would be "a vote on gun control."[96]

10

What Are the Alternatives?

Any realistic evaluation of the gun issue must take into account several indisputable facts. First, according to a December 1993 report by the federal Bureau of Alcohol, Tobacco and Firearms, there are at least 211 million guns, including 71 million handguns, in private hands in this country. Second, thanks to the frequent use of lethal weapons in the commission of crimes, retail sales of guns purchased for personal protection are on the rise. Third, reverence for the Constitution, plus the unceasing propaganda of gun organizations, sustain the mistaken but widespread belief that the Second Amendment guarantees every individual the right to keep and bear arms. Notwithstanding this general impression, every public opinion poll taken over the past fifty years shows approximately 75 percent of the people in favor of some form of gun control. Finally, the cult of violence that pervades every aspect of American life, from daily news features to the entertainment industry to the conduct of foreign affairs, poses the greatest threat to law and order since the Civil War.[1]

The very existence of 211 million guns in a nation of 250 million people demonstrates that gun control—in the sense of a regulatory system that will provide a record of the production, distribution, sale and resale of every firearm, plus a reliable procedure for screening out would-be purchasers who are not legally entitled to own firearms—can no longer be achieved solely by the kind of legislation proposed by gun-control advocates. Those who are seriously concernerd about this problem must begin to think of long-term solutions that take into consideration the country's total experience with firearms.

This is not to say that a ban on Saturday night specials and private ownership of assault weapons would not be useful. But this would be only a first step. Other important reforms are necessary. One is the development of a nationwide information network of the kind suggested by progun Representative Harley O. Staggers of West Virginia. His suggestion was to set up a "toll-free hotline that firearms dealers could contact to learn if the handgun purchaser is prohibited by federal law from possessing a handgun."[2] Offered as a substitute for the Brady bill, this measure was intended to affect handgun purchases only. However, the same system could be applied to the purchase of any firearm or any particular type of weapon.

Staggers's plan was rejected in a test vote, but it was later included in the House-Senate Conference Committee's compromise bill, which proposed putting the Brady waiting period into effect until "the national instant criminal background check system is established."[3] This took into acount the Office of Technology Assessment's estimate that it would take "five to ten years" to develop such a system.[4]

Thanks to President Bush's condemnation of the limits placed on his habeas corpus and exclusionary rule reforms, which in turn incited a progun filibuster of the compromise in the Senate, this comprehensive crime-control legislation died in 1992. Insofar as the gun-control section is concerned, a subsequent bill along the lines of the Brady-Staggers compromise was ultimately adopted and signed into law by President Clinton. When, at Clinton's urging, Congress approved the further restriction on the continued production and sale of a variety of assault weapons, it was over the strong opposition of progun organizations, whose objectives were twofold. One argument was that, at least for semiautomatic weapons, there is little to distinguish a hunting rifle from a military piece. The other was that this type of legislation is merely one step on the road to outlawing all private ownership of guns.

On the first point, they were technically correct. An ordinary repeating rifle might fire the same kind of ammunition, at the same muzzle velocity, with the same deadly effect, as a semiautomatic weapon designed for military use. But the repeater could not be mounted with a magazine holding fifty or more cartridges, and it could not be converted to fully automatic fire. Progunners insist this conversion is not easily done with semiautomatics. However, as indicated earlier, do-it-yourself manuals for converting military style semiautomatics to automatic fire are available to anyone who wishes to buy them. And as more than one hunter has pointed out, such weapons have no place in a hunter's arsenal.[5]

Further removed from reality is the repeated NRA charge that the ultimate aim of gun control advocates "is to get rid of every firearm in the hands of every law-abiding citizen in this nation."[6] Whether it is an expression of a sincere belief or merely a scare tactic to incite readers of this message to line up in opposition to any kind of control is immaterial. The fact is that only those on the outer fringe of the control faction go to this extreme. The great majority of the general public, including organizations like Handgun Control and the National Coalition to Ban Handguns, take no such position, recognizing the legitimacy of the demand for the kinds of weapons ordinarily used for hunting and target shooting. When NCBH went to court to challenge the government's policy of making surplus M-1 army rifles available to NRA members only, it was in effect demanding that sales of these guns (at cost) be open to any qualified person, whether affiliated with NRA or not.[7] Moreover, public opinion polls that show an overwhelming majority of people favoring more gun control also reveal that this desire is based on the rising crime rate and the fear for personal safety; it reflects no antipathy toward hunting and target shooting.[8]

The most far-reaching proposal would not dispossess any individual of any legitimate hunting or target-shooting weapon. It would, however, require every newly manufactured firearm to be identified by manufacturer's serial number and to be registered in the name of the dealer and/or purchaser of the weapon. This approach is no different from the one that has become traditional in dealing with automotive vehicles, with all fifty states requiring not only the registration of each vehicle but the licensing of every driver. The most ardent advocate of Second Amendment rights has yet to protest this intrusion into the private life of automobile owners. Nor is there any evidence that progunners believe dangerous drugs should be freely available without a doctor's prescription certifying to the user's need for such medication.

Legislation requiring the licensing of every gun owner and the registration of every weapon manufactured here or imported from abroad would not affect owners of the 211 million guns presently in private hands. Nor should the law be made retroactive, as the task of registering so enormous and widely distributed a quantity of weapons would be an impossible one, and the effort to do so would create so much ill will that the prospect of more effective federal control would be destroyed. Rather, the objective should be to create a mechanism that, over the long haul, would bring order out of the chaos of conflicting state laws and heretofore ineffective federal regulation.

The alternative is to muddle along with patchwork remedies that will neither reduce the number of gun-related deaths—homicidal, accidental or suicidal—nor impede the flow of firearms throughout the nation from states with few controls. And if the estimated annual increase of four million privately purchased guns continues, by the end of this decade there will be almost as many guns as people in these United States.

Another aspect of the problem is identification of persons ineligible to purchase or possess firearms. Bush's Attorney General Dick Thornburgh took a step in the direction suggested by Staggers. He did this in responding to an instruction contained in the Anti–Drug Abuse Act of 1988, which required the attorney general to report to Congress on "a system for the immediate and accurate identification of felons who attempt to purchase firearms" and "to conduct a study to determine if an effective method exists for the immediate and accurate identification of other persons who attempt to purchase firearms but are ineligible to do so because they fall into other categories created by the Gun Control Act of 1968."[9]

Some progress has been made in designing a system of criminal identification. A survey of the criminal history records of all fifty states and the District of Columbia was completed in 1991. This study revealed that 60 percent of the criminal history records maintained by state agencies are automated. As automation is adopted by other states, the Justice Department will come closer to achieving its proposed goal of establishing a system in which gun dealers can inquire by telephone or computer terminal as to the eligibility of a purchaser and receive an immediate response. The weakness of the proposed system is that it would be based upon adoption by the states of "voluntary reporting standards" recommended by the FBI. Further, it is concerned only with the identification and registration of criminals, not guns, which points up the parallel need for gun registration.

The more complex problem of identifying persons other than felons who are ineligible to purchase firearms was turned over to a private organization for study. The 1990 report of that company, the ENFORTH Corporation, found so many difficulties in establishing legally who are "unlawful users of controlled substances," or "mentally defective," or "illegal aliens," that little progress can be expected in this area.[10]

Any further discussion of the role of the Second Amendment would seem needless, except for one seemingly contradictory aspect of the general public's view of the gun problem. Notwithstanding the consistency with which the desire for stronger controls has been expressed over more than fifty years of opinion polling, the effectiveness of the gun lobby's endless repetition of the Second Amendment theme has convinced a substantial majority of people to respond affirmatively to the question, "Would you happen to know, is the right to own a gun guaranteed by the Constitution or not?" Asked this question in May 1991, 77 percent said Yes and only 9 percent said No, the remaining 14 percent either being uncertain or having no opinion.[11]

This impression was fostered not only by gun clubs but by members of national and state legislatures, most of whom, as lawyers, should know better. Indeed, it is reasonable to assume that many—especially those in Congress—do know better, being fully familiar with the series of Supreme Court decisions that refute the assertion that the Second Amendment guarantees every individual the right to keep and bear arms. Three of the five senators who signed a minority statement that helped defeat the Anti-drug, Assault Weapons Limitation Act of 1989 were lawyers with a thorough understanding of the constitutional issues. One of the three—South Carolina's Strom Thurmond—had been admitted to practice in every federal court, including the Supreme Court of the United States. Yet Thurmond joined Charles E. Grassley of Iowa, Gordon J. Humphrey of New Hampshire and lawyers Orrin Hatch of Utah and Alan K. Simpson of Wyoming in asserting that the proposed act "represents another attempt to infringe on the constitutional right to keep and bear arms."[12]

The same misstatement of fact has been heard on many occasions in the House of Representatives. Just as often, the issue is confused by a representative comparing the gun situation with some other that has no relevance whatever. In debating the choice between the Brady bill and the Staggers substitute, Robert S. Walker of Pennsylvania suggested that telling a handgun purchaser he must wait 7 days before taking possession of the weapon would be like telling a newspaper editor, "If you are going to spread pornography in our society, you have to apply 7 days in advance and tell us what it is you are going to do, and then we will decide whether or not you are a criminal."[13] Later in the discussion, Representative Staggers demonstrated how easy it is to misconstrue the philosophy behind the movement for gun control. Attacking the Brady bill, he said, "A 7-day waiting period is a simplistic answer," adding, "In the same logic, if we would wait, say, 7 days to purchase cocaine, we could solve the drug problem."[14] In both cases the purpose of controlling legislation is to ensure that the purchaser is entitled to obtain and use a dangerous product. Staggers gave no indication, here or elsewhere, that he supported the view that the drug problem would be resolved by eliminating all controls over the production, sale and use of cocaine, morphine, crack and so forth. Yet this is "the same logic" that underlies his—and the gun lobby's—demand that all gun-control laws be eliminated.

Walker's assertion that the Second Amendment provides the same kind of protection for gun owners as the First Amendment does for people claiming freedom of speech is another argument frequently heard in Congress. During the debate over the choice between the Brady and Staggers bills, Representative Jolene Unsoeld of Washington spoke of "basic rights such as free speech, or free exercise of religion, a woman's right of choice or the right to keep and bear arms," as though all were equally unqualified.[15] In fact, two centuries of experience, confirmed by Supreme Court decisions, has established limits even for the freedoms guaranteed by the First Amendment. Freedom of speech, for example, does not extend to the individual who creates panic by falsely shouting "Fire" in a crowded theater. The free exercise of religion does not permit forcing worshippers to handle poisonous snakes.

These limitations are not specified in the First Amendment, but other sections of the Bill of Rights have built-in limitations. The Third Amendment's ban on quartering soldiers in private homes does not apply if in time of war laws are passed to permit such an invasion of privacy. Similarly, "the right of the people to be secure in their persons, houses, papers and effects" is conditioned by the Fourth Amendment's further provision that this applied only to "unreasonable" searches and seizures, and that a search warrant may be issued "upon probable cause, supported by Oath or affirmation, and particularly describing the place to be searched, and the persons or things to be seized." In this connection, it is interesting to note that the most vehement defenders of the right to keep and bear arms are frequently supporters of proposals—like those of President George Bush—that would weaken the Fourth Amendment by giving police greater latitude in conducting searches with or without warrants, just so long as those tactics are not used against gun owners or dealers.[16]

Just as other amendments specify the limits of their application, the Second Amendment establishes an important limit on the right to keep and bear arms by asserting that its purpose is to provide for "a well regulated Militia." As demonstrated in an earlier chapter, the militia that was so essential to national defense during the early days of the Republic has been replaced by an enormous professional standing army of the sort that would not have been tolerated by the authors of the Second Amendment. Organizations like the National Rifle Association, the Second Amendment Foundation, and the Citizens' Committee for the Right to Keep and Bear Arms insist that the militia still exists in the National Guard and, more broadly, in an armed citizenry. But that view is no longer heard in Congress, even from members who argue against the imposition of federal gun controls. Even the NRA assumption that gun clubs help prepare people for military service carries little weight in an era in which the changing technology of war has made instruction in rifle and pistol shooting far less significant than the highly technical training required of pilots, navigators, submariners and operators of complex defense and weapons systems.

Popular acceptance of the notion that the Second Amendment guarantees everyone the right to keep and bear arms is less a barrier to legislative reform than the pervasive violence that infects American society. In a foreword to the FBI's *Uniform Crime Reports* for 1990, Director William S. Sessions wrote: "As we proceed into the 21st century, the foremost challenge of the law enforcement community is its continued success in the warfare against the escalating violent crime occurrences in the United States."[17] Disregarding the implied boast that law enforcement agencies have been winning the war against crimes of violence, the reader is struck by the acknowledgment that such activity was still on the increase near the close of an administration presumably dedicated to instilling a kinder, gentler spirit in the American way of life.

Equally alarming is the fact that most of the remaining intro-
ductory paragraphs are devoted to the growing need to devote
more attention to "hate-related offenses . . . crimes motivated by
prejudice against a victim's race, religion, ethnic origin or sexual
orientation." The bureau's decision to begin classifying crimes
under this heading was necessitated by passage of the Hate Crime
Statistics Act of 1990, which Sessions says resulted from concern
in Congress "that the degree of prejudice-motivated crimes in
America during the 1980s had increased dramatically."[18]

No expertise in crime control is needed to demonstrate the extent
to which violence has become a major force in American life. The
average citizen sees the evidence in the featured story in almost
every television newscast, in nearly every daily newspaper, and in
the steady diet of films featuring Rambo-type heroes whose major
talent is killing. And because the evidence is pressed upon the
public day in and day out, it invades the minds of children as well
as adults, telling them, in effect, that their world is one in which
violence commands more attention, even more respect, than non-
violence, and the gun toter reigns supreme.

California provides a showcase for the way in which violence has
come to dominate everyday life. In the aftermath of President
Kennedy's assassination, California adopted a 15-day waiting
period for the purchase of any concealable handgun. Following the
Stockton massacre, it approved the Roberti-Roos Assault Weapons
Act of 1989.[19] But in between these actions a more strict handgun
control measure was defeated by a vote in which 63 percent disap-
proved when the proposal was put on the ballot as an initiative in
the election of 1982.[20] And through this entire period the state was
(and continues to be) the home of one of the country's major
manufacturers of Saturday night specials.[21]

A 1992 sequence of events brought home both the accuracy of the
FBI director's assessment of rising violence and the fallacy of his
assertion that the war against violence is being won. In quick
succession: Los Angeles police reacted to a minor misdemeanor
with a savage attack on the culprit, this act by white police officers
against a black suspect was given the stamp of approval by a jury
selected in a white suburb far from the inner city where the arrest
took place, outraged blacks went on a rampage in which lives were
lost and stores looted and destroyed, and immediately the sale of
guns for self-protection skyrocketed to the highest rate known to
record-keeping authorities.[22]

Even as the FBI director's 1990 report was going to press, efforts were being made in New York to ban private possession of all assault weapons. Six experts were asked by the *New York Times* to suggest measures for bringing street violence under control. Four of the six simply repeated in a variety of ways the recommendations that gun laws be made more strict and/or that penalties be made more severe. One suggested that, because of the strong tie between the illegal drug trade and the many killings that trade produced, it might be desirable to consider decriminalizing the use of drugs. Only one expressed the view that "gun control alone won't help," recommending more widespread use of an experimental program that appears to reduce teenage battles by having students mediate the disputes that arise among their schoolmates.[23]

Only this last suggestion comes close to the heart of the problem, which is to wean the country away from the gun culture that has evolved to a point at which even children are led to believe that a gun brings recognition, status and fulfillment. This cannot be accomplished by legislation, although the previously recommended measures for curtailing further proliferation of privately owned weapons would put the public on notice as to the seriousness of the government's intentions.

In this connection, it is important that the laws governing the sale of guns include a provision mandating a course of training and testing for each purchaser. Here we can learn from other countries. New Zealand, for example, makes certain that every purchaser is thoroughly familiar with both the gun-control laws and the proper handling of his or her weapon, providing a detailed manual for that purpose and administering a written examination before permitting the purchase to be completed.

Change cannot be effected merely by adopting the practices of a culture different from our own, but surely we can learn from the experience of others, particularly from a country like New Zealand, whose language is the same as ours and whose pioneer background is in many ways similar to our own.

Evidence that the notion of a training requirement has gained acceptance in the United States is seen in the January 1994 monthly report of a Gallup Poll in which 89 percent of those questioned— and 82 percent of gun owners—agreed that to qualify for gun ownership gun buyers should be required to take safety classes.

Another aspect of the problem is the concept of personal responsibility and accountability on the part of gun owners. The importance of this principle has begun to penetrate the legislative mind, as in Florida. In June 1989 that state's legislature met in special session to deal with the increasing incidence of accidental shootings by children using guns that had not been properly protected by their owners. The lawmakers' reaction to this dangerous trend was made clear by their approval of a bill that states its findings in these terms:

The Legislature finds that a tragically large number of Florida children have been accidentally killed or seriously injured by negligently stored firearms; that placing firearms within the reach or easy access of children is irresponsible, encourages such accidents, and should be prohibited; and that legislative action is necessary to protect the safety of our children.

Disavowing any intent to deny adult citizens "their constitutional right to keep and bear firearms for hunting and sporting activities and for defense of self, family, home and business and as collectibles," the lawmakers made it a misdemeanor to leave a loaded firearm within easy access of a minor and a felony if the minor injures or kills someone with that weapon.[24]

The first of three cases tried under this revolutionary statute involved a 14-year-old boy who found his father's pistol on a closet shelf and, while showing it to a friend, accidentally shot him in the head. Although the wounded boy did not die, he lost the sight of one eye. Because of conflicting testimony as to who had loaded the gun, a jury found the father guilty of a misdemeanor rather than a felony. That decision was later upheld by a judge, who sentenced the father to six months' probation.[25]

Light as this sentence was, successful prosecution of the case set an important precedent that did not go unnoticed in other states. By mid-1993, what came to be known as "child accident prevention" laws had been passed by California, Connecticut, Illinois, Maryland, New Jersey, Wisconsin and the cities of Baltimore, Cleveland and Houston. In California, a father lost his 4-year-old son when the boy killed himself with a pistol the father had left in his bedroom, still loaded, after using it to celebrate the new year. Criminally liable under the new California law, the distraught father willingly accepted a misdemeanor sentence that included an obligation to make radio and television appeals to other parents to avoid careless handling of firearms.[26]

Florida set another precedent when in the November 1990 election 84 percent of the voters approved an amendment to the state constitution that requires a 3-day waiting period and a criminal background check prior to the purchase of a handgun. While state and local police expressed doubts about the deterrent effect on criminals, the fact that for the first time a state had written the waiting-period principle into its constitution indicates the degree of concern felt by the general public over the rising rate of deaths by firearms.[27]

Implementing the constitutional mandate, Florida established a requirement that gun dealers telephone for an instant computer search of criminal records at the National Crime Information Center and Florida Crime Information Center while a gun customer is in the store. According to state officials, these checks take an average of a little more than 3 minutes and, in the first six months of the program, revealed criminal records that resulted in rejection of 2,908 of the 108,042 requests to purchase a firearm.[28]

In some parts of the country the gun-toting tradition is so deeply rooted that acceptance of the Florida approach will be difficult to achieve. When 13- and 14-year-old gang members attended a meeting held by the mayor of Phoenix, Arizona, "with guns strapped to their hips," city officials were aghast. They were even more perturbed to learn that the youngsters' actions were entirely legal. City authorities reacted by passing an ordinance that would bar minors from carrying guns without their parents' permission.[29] Whether or not this restriction will survive the legal challenge threatened by the NRA is, as of this writing, uncertain. The only restriction in Arizona state law affecting minors is one that prohibits the sale or gift of a firearm to a minor "without written consent of the minor's parent or legal guardian." The law says nothing that would suggest a minor does not have the same right as an adult, who in that state needs no license to carry a gun openly. Moreover, Arizona has a preemption clause that states: "A political subdivision of this state shall not require the licensing or registration of firearms or prohibit the ownership, purchase, sale or transfer of firearms."[30]

It is this kind of permissiveness in the treatment of firearms that disturbs—even frightens—many people who view the trend toward increasing violence as a serious threat to the internal security of the nation. That concern was expressed by the leaders of the medical profession in a special issue of the *Journal of the American Medical Association*. In nineteen separate articles, the journal painted a picture of violence in America that a concluding editorial characterized as "a public health emergency."[31]

Not infrequently, control advocates point to the experience of countries with strict gun laws and far lower crime rates, particularly in the homicide category, and suggest that the United States would do well to adopt their practices. But this is more easily said than done. The most powerful influence mitigating against acceptance of, for example, the British system is tradition. From the earliest period of colonization on this continent, guns were essential to the survival of the settlers. Without guns they would have been incapable of defending themselves against attacks by colonial forces of other countries and by Native Americans, who quite correctly saw these newcomers as trespassers on their lands. Without guns, and lacking the Indians' hunting skills with bow and arrow, many settlers would have starved for lack of food, particularly during the long months required to raise food crops. These two problems of defense and food supply persisted as settlers moved farther and farther west.

It is true that the early pioneers in Canada, Australia and New Zealand faced conditions that were similar in many respects to those in the United States, although in the South Pacific the British faced much less competition from the European empires that strenuously resisted their claims in North America. Other differences were equally important, particularly in Australia, which Britain used as a penal colony from the first settlement of convicts in 1788 until the last group was landed in New South Wales in 1840.

With a current population of only 17 million people and a land area almost as large as the continental United States, the vast spaces of Australia—much of it desert or rocky, arid terrain—continue to attract people of adventurous spirit. Settling initially along the eastern shore, the westward-moving pioneers have had the same need for weapons as the Americans who left the safety of the original thirteen colonies to seek opportunities farther west.

As in Australia, New Zealand settlers depended upon their weapons for both protection and food. Unlike Australia, New Zealand was never used as a penal colony. Moreover, its occupation by emigrants from the British Isles was for many years discouraged by the government. Fierce resistance by the native Maoris added to the hazards of colonization and made guns a necessity for protection as well as for hunting food.

A mountainous area the size of Colorado, New Zealand presented a challenging terrain to its colonists. Possession and use of guns came as naturally to New Zealanders as to American pioneers. Yet the island nation developed without the "wild West" tradition that in many parts of nineteenth-century America produced an atmosphere in which gun law and lynch law were not uncommon. As described earlier, twentieth-century New Zealand has developed a uniquely efficient system of control for private ownership of weapons that is probably superior to that of any other democratic nation.

Canada's development more closely parallels that of the United States. Like the United States, its early years were filled with struggles of two varieties, to establish permanent colonies in a new and hostile land, and to survive the repeated wars between England and France for domination of the area. Under these circumstances, it is understandable that guns in the hands of the settlers were as common as in the United States.

As indicated earlier, modern Canada has taken the problem of gun control far more seriously than the United States.[32] As anti-control advocates in the U.S. Congress and the White House were doing their best to water down or eliminate the modest restrictions enacted in 1968, the Canadian Parliament and Justice Department commissioned a private corporation to study the impact of its first major change in the firearms section of its criminal code. When that study showed that murders, accidents and suicides with firearms all declined after passage of the 1977 legislation, it seemed clear that statutory controls were having a beneficial effect.

Public support for this approach was widespread. A nationwide poll conducted by the *Toronto Star* indicated that 70 percent of all Canadians believed the law should be made even more restrictive. On the strength of this public support, Parliament in 1991 further strengthened its controls, among other things extending the classification of "prohibited weapon" from automatics to semi-automatics by adding to the prohibition of an automatic weapon the clause, "whether or not it has been altered to fire only one projectile with one such pressure [on the trigger]."[33]

What we learn from other countries is not the art of drafting control legislation; it is recognition of the different results that stem from an open market in gun traffic as compared with a system of controls that in no way interferes with the activities of hunters, target shooters and gun collectors, but draws a clear line between

legitimate and illegitimate weaponry and between responsible
and irresponsible weapon owners. Every opinion poll taken over
the last half century demonstrates that the American public is
aware of the need to make these distinctions. But the combination
of gutlessness among many of our legislators and the fraudulent
representation of the Second Amendment as a guarantee of the
right ot keep and bear arms—by legislators and gun lobbyists
alike—has frustrated the public will. It is tempting to propose
removing this excuse by repeal of the Second Amendment as an
outdated anachronism. But that would lend credence to the argument that gun-control advocates are out to destroy the Bill of
Rights.

The situation is further complicated by the rising friction between ethnic and religious groups. Like a global epidemic, we
read almost daily about the slaughter of Kurds by Iraqis, of
Bosnians by Serbs, of Armenians by Azerbaijanis and Azerbaijanis
by Armenians, of Muslims by Hindus and Hindus by Muslims, of
Burundi's Hutu civilians by Tutsi soldiers. And much as we hate
to admit it, the infection has made its appearance in the United
States as well, though on a smaller scale.

Like AIDS, hate is a disease that is difficult to control and even
more difficult to cure. It cannot be legislated out of existence. In a
society that is truly free, it cannot be made illegal. It could be
attacked through an educational program aimed at all ages in all
segments of society. But the American educational system is not
geared to such an effort. Moreover, at the high school and college
levels education is commonly seen as having the more practical
objective of preparing young people to meet the immediate challenges of everyday life—like earning a living and learning how to
improve one's economic and social position in a highly competitive
society.

One of the greatest impediments to freedom in the learning
process is the attitude of leaders like the Great Communicator. As
governor of California, Ronald Reagan denounced federal aid to
education as "the foot in the door to federal control." On the other
hand, he proposed that college faculty should be required "to be
proponents of those ethical and moral standards demanded by the
great majority of our society"—meaning those he preached but did
little to carry out.[34]

To the extent to which ethnic, religious and racial prejudices
influence choices made in providing jobs, housing, education and

the luxuries of life, a listless economy and the growing disparity between rich and poor tend to foster the very prejudices that for much of this country's history kept minority ethnics and nonwhite races in inferior positions. White ethnic and religious groups such as Irish and Italian immigrants, Jews and Mormons eventually won the battle against discrimination. But the same cannot be said of nonwhites. After a period of progress beginning with the Supreme Court's 1954 decision in Brown v. Board of Education, the old antagonisms began to rise again. Thanks in part to twelve years of resistance to civil rights legislation by the Reagan and Bush administrations, and their efforts in support of both business and religious institutions attempting to evade the laws against discrimination, racial and religious hostilities have become more virulent. Administration toleration of business and market practices in which greed outweighed ethical considerations also encouraged a get-what-you-can-any-way-you-can attitude in all levels of society.

In the competition for recognition, political power and economic advancement, violent clashes between whites and nonwhites, between Jews and blacks and between Jews and Christians[35] occur with increasing frequency. Even among black, Hispanic and Asian groups, a 1994 survey by Louis Harris found that these minorities "resent one another almost as much as they do whites." And the murder of two Japanese students visiting Los Angeles, while not ascribed to racial animosity, reinforced opinion in Japan that the United States is a "gun society."[36]

When added to the open warfare between law enforcement agencies and both organized and unorganized crime, these ethnic animosities often extend the practice of gunplay to communities, large and small, in every part of the country. This spurs even further the demand for guns, even by normally nonviolent people, who fear for their own and their families' safety. The pity of it is that after twelve years of federal government emphasis on law and order, there is more crime, more violence, more fear than ever before. Even passage of the Brady bill had the unfortunate side effect of inducing people who never contemplated owning a gun to scurry to the nearest gunshop to secure a weapon before tighter controls could be applied.[37]

No significant change in the character of a society can occur without a change in attitude. But except where the pressures are so great as to produce a nationwide revolt, social change is a long, slow process. It took this country two centuries to arrive at a democratic society in which men and women of all races and creeds are acknowledged to be entitled to the same rights and privileges under the law. Nevertheless, the widespread poverty, competition for jobs and the divisive forces of racial, religious and ethnic animosity that encourage violence presage a bleak future—at least in the short term.

One hopeful sign is a shift in opinion regarding gun control where it counts most—in the state and local legislatures of the country. As indicated earlier, the movement to contain the proliferation of gun sales began at the grassroots level, with town and city fathers responding to the growing threat by heeding the long-standing public preference and passing laws to control the sale of firearms. State legislatures have been more reluctant to adopt such laws, but by 1993 a trend away from the laissez faire posture of the past has become noticeable. The New Jersey legislature, which in 1990 banned the private purchase of military assault-type weapons, was pressured by the NRA into reversing that action at the next session. However, despite an all-out effort by the NRA in support of repeal, the Senate failed to override Governor Florio's veto of the repeal bill. Senators who had formerly adhered strictly to the NRA point of view were swayed by repeated incidents in which innocent children, civilians and police officers had been killed by gunfire. California also banned the sale of assault weapons to the general public, followed by Connecticut, where pressure from both the NRA and Colt Manufacturing Company, a major arms producer, failed to deter state lawmakers from approving a law banning the sale of a variety of semiautomatic assault weapons, including the Colt Sporter.[38]

Significant actions were taken in other states as well. Hawaii was the first state to use a generic definition of assault weapons, although its ban applies only to assault pistols and pistol "ammunition magazines holding more than ten rounds." Both Louisiana and Missouri rejected proposals that would have permitted their citizens to carry concealed weapons. And Virginia, a major source of weapons ending up in New York, responded to pleas from New York officials by passing a law that curtails the previously unlimited purchase of guns "by the trunkful," restricting Virginia residents' purchases of guns to one a month. Even in Pennsylvania, where military-style rifles can be purchased on a walk-in basis by anyone holding an easily obtained gun permit, a Republican representative submitted a bill that would require a 48-hour waiting period and background check prior to the purchase of this type of weapon. Two months later, in June 1993, Philadelphia banned further sale of military-style assault guns.[39]

Finally, a willingness to support control legislation appeared at the federal level when President Clinton told a joint session of Congress, "If you will pass the Brady bill, I'll sign it."[40] Subsequently, two government agencies that normally refrain from offering opinions on either side of a policy question came out publicly in support of a waiting period for handgun purchases. Stephen Higgins, director of the federal Bureau of Alcohol, Tobacco and Firearms (BATF), cited the Waco, Texas, shoot-out as the reason for this departure from standard practice, saying, "We've never had four agents killed on a single day before." Later that year, FBI Director William S. Sessions reversed the stand he had been obliged to take under Presidents Reagan and Bush and publicly acknowledged having sent Attorney General Janet Reno a set of proposals that included a 5-day waiting period for the purchase of a handgun.[41]

Violence has become so much a part of everyday life in these United States that, as with drug use, the admonition to "just say no" will not be sufficient to produce any substantial change. Nor will gun-control legislation by itself accomplish this. The remedy—part conceptual, part economic—depends on the kind of public and private leadership that will devote whatever time and money it takes to convince both the adult and juvenile population of the need for reversing the perception, fostered by an endless stream of Rambo-type movies and war stories that focus almost exclusively on the heroics rather than the horror of mass killing, that "a nation's values and its greatness spring from the barrel of a gun."[42]

An equally compelling need is to heal the racial, religious and ethnic tensions that threaten to disrupt other efforts at recovery from the low state of morale, health and economic well-being felt by so large a segment of the population.

The task is not solely one of education, although this is crucial to success, nor is it only to reestablish a nationwide sense of harmony, but the task is to broaden opportunities for the 40 percent of American children living at the poverty level and to bring this nation back to a competitive position with other industrialized countries, most notably Germany and Japan. This also means placing as high a priority on health, education and job opportunities for all adults as on millitary needs and budget reduction.

Presidential candidate Franklin D. Roosevelt reminded voters in 1932 that the multitudes represented by "the forgotten man at the bottom of the economic pyramid" must be the foundation on which a nation builds its economy and its strength. Part of that building process turns on the availability of adequate educational opportunities for the forgotten man's children. Those opportunities have been made more difficult to attain by the violence that has penetrated even into the classroom. The Gun Violence Prevention Act of 1994 (S. 1882) cited this as one of the conditions that call for tighter controls, declaring: "the occurrence of gun violence in schools has resulted in a decline in the quality of education in our country and this, in turn, has an adverse impact on interstate commerce and the foreign commerce of the United States."[43]

Three-quarters of a century ago, H. G. Wells wrote, "Human history becomes more and more a race between education and catastrophe."[44] That was never more true than it is today.

Notes

Care has been taken to document every quotation or reference to the opinion of every individual or organization mentioned in the text. The most frequently used sources are cited in the abbreviated form shown below. For other sources, the author and title are given in full in the first citation and in abbreviated form thereafter. All documents and publications cited in the text are included in the bibliography that follows immediately after the notes.

CR, *Congressional Record*. If reference is to the daily, unbound issues, the citation will be: CR (daily) plus date and page number.

H.R., U.S. House of Representatives.

NYT, *New York Times*

P.L., Public Law, followed by number and either date of enactment or volume and page in *U.S. Statutes at Large* or *U.S. Code*

PPP, *Public Papers of the Presidents of the United States*

WCPD, *Weekly Compilation of Presidential Documents*

WP, *Washington Post*

CHAPTER 1: OUR EUROPEAN HERITAGE

1. Stephen P. Halbrook, *That Every Man Be Armed: The Evolution of a Constitutional Right*, chap. 1.
2. Ibid., p. x.

3. Halbrook, pp. 20–24; Charles S. Hyneman and Donald S. Lutz, eds., *American Political Writing during the Founding Era 1760–1805*, vol. 1, pp. 14, 94, 359, 598; Library of Congress, *Letters of Delegates to Congress, 1774–1789*, vol. 3, p. 44; Niccolò Machiavelli, *The Prince.*

4. Halbrook, p. 7 ; Jefferson to Henry Lee, 8 May 1825, in Merrill D. Peterson, ed., *Thomas Jefferson: Writings*, p. 1501.

5. Peterson, p. 1242. For references to Montesquieu by other revolutionary leaders, most of them more flattering than Jefferson's, see Bernard Schwartz, ed., *The Roots of the Bill of Rights*, vol. 1, p. 224, vol. 3, p. 608, vol. 4, pp. 667, 763. Many more can be found in Hyneman and Lutz.

6. PPP, 1982, pp. 473–74.

7. Basil Thomson, *The Story of Scotland Yard*, pp. 17–18.

8. Ibid., pp. 20–21.

9. Ibid., p. 87.

10. Ibid., p. 91.

11. WCPD, 23 March 1986, pp. 406–7.

12. Thomson, p. 332.

13. Peter Laurie, *Scotland Yard: A Study of the Metropolitan Police*, pp. 73–74.

14. For more on Reagan's qualifications as a historian, see Wilbur Edel, *The Reagan Presidency*, chap. 4.

15. Robert E. Shalope, "The Ideological Origins of the Second Amendment," *Journal of American History* (December 1982), p. 602.

16. Edward Dumbault, *The Bill of Rights*, p. 168.

17. Halbrook, p. 90.

18. Ibid., p. 91.

19. Every high school or college textbook on American history includes one or more chapters on the colonial period. A greater appreciation for the tenor of the times just prior to the Revolution can be gained from the opinions of people living in that era. See, for example the collection of speeches, sermons, letters and newspaper articles in Henry Steele Commager and Richard B. Morris, *The Spirit of Seventy-Six*, chaps. 1–4; Library of Congress, vols. 1–4; Schwartz, vol. 1; Paul H. Smith, comp., *English Defenders of American Freedom 1774–1778.*

CHAPTER 2: GUNS AND THE CONSTITUTION

1. Schwartz, vol. 1, p. 49.

2. Hyneman and Lutz, vol. 1, p. 46. The Magna Carta was an agreement the British barons forced upon King John in 1215, principally for their own protection but including an acknowledgment that the liberties listed in the Carta (charter) applied to "all freemen" in the kingdom.

3. Henry Steele Commager and Milton Cantor, *Documents of American History*, 10th ed., vol. 1, p. 45.

4. Hyneman and Lutz, vol. 1, p. 106.

5. Ibid., pp. 198–99.

6. Maurice Matloff, ed., *American Military History*, rev. ed., p. 28.

7. Ibid., p. 29.

8. The message from Congress, approved 10 May 1776 and published 15 May, recommended that the colonies "adopt such governments as shall in the opinion of the Representatives of the People best conduce to the happiness and safety of their constituents in particular, and America in general." See Library of Congress, *Letters*, vol. 3, p. 677. Reproductions of the colonial charters and early state constitutions are contained in Ben Perley Poore, comp., *The Federal and State Constitutions, Colonial Charters, and Other Organic Laws of the United States.*

9. Richard Henry Lee's recommendation was included in the resolution calling for a declaration of independence. That resolution and the draft Articles of Confederation produced by Josiah Bartlett of New Hampshire and John Dickenson of Pennsylvania are reproduced in Library of Congress, *Letters*, vol. 4, pp. 157, 233–50. For the version finally adopted, see Charles C. Tansill, ed., *Documents Illustrative of the Formation of the Union of American States*, pp. 27–37.

10. Library of Congress, *Letters*, vol. 4, p. 234 and n.3, p. 253.

11. Tansill, p. 29.

12. Jonathan Elliot, ed., *The Debates in the Several Conventions on the Adoption of the Federal Constitution as Recommended by the General Convention at Philadelphia in 1787*, 2nd ed., vol. 1, p. 115.

13. Tansill, pp. 29–30.

14. Ibid., pp. 27–28.

15. Library of Congress, *Letters*, vol. 14, p. 470.

16. Ibid., vol. 15, pp. 454–56.

17. Ibid., vol. 16, p. 648.

18. Ibid., vol. 17, p. 117.

19. Arguments against acceptance of the Constitution of 1787 are detailed in Jackson Turner Main, *The Anti-Federalists: Critics of the Constitution, 1781–1788.*

20. Tansill, p. 716.

21. Ibid., pp. 698, 701, 737, 951.

22. Ibid., pp. 567–71.

23. Ibid., pp. 564, 567–71, 598–603, 621, 666.

24. Ibid., pp. 725–26.

25. The first five ratifications came from Delaware on 7 December 1787, Pennsylvania on 12 December 1787, New Jersey on 18 December 1787, Georgia on 2 January 1788 and Connecticut on 9 January 1788. See Tansill, pp. 1009–17.

26. John P. Kaminski and Gaspare J. Saladino, eds., *The Documentary History of the Ratification of the Constitution*, vol. 8, p. 14. Hamilton was a member of the New York delegation in Congress as well as a delegate to the Constitutional Convention.

27. Ibid., vol. 13, p. 231.

28. Ibid., pp. 232–33.

29. Ibid., p. 241.

30. Elliot, vol. 2, pp. 408, 489–99. It should be noted that Elliot's *Debates* contain none of the speeches made in the Pennsylvania convention by opponents of the Constitution. Volume 2, pp. 503–4 does, however, reproduce a petition recommending a number of amendments to the Constitution, including requirements that two-thirds of Congress must approve a peacetime standing army and that

federal control of the militia must be limited to two months unless a longer term was approved by the state legislature.

31. For an analysis of the opposition, see Main, especially pp. 158–61, on the demand for a bill of rights.

32. Elliot, vol. 2, p. 184.

33. Ibid., vol. 1, pp. 531–33.

34. Ibid., vol. 2, p. 533; vol. 3, pp. 592–94.

35. Tansill, p. 533; Eliot, vol. 3, pp. 82, 302, 411, 425.

36. Tansill, p. 1026.

37. Ibid., pp. 1030–34, 1035, 1044–51, 1052–59.

38. Dumbault, chap. 1; Schwartz, vol. 3, pp. 592, 606–7, 615–17.

39. This pledge was repeated a number of times in letters to constituents. See Robert A. Rutland, ed., *The Papers of James Madison*, vol. 11, pp. 405, 416, 428.

40. Schwartz, vol. 5, pp. 1006–9, 1016–34, 1121–23, 1145–47, 1159–61. Madison's speech introducing his proposed amendments to Congress is reported in Rutland, vol. 12, pp. 196–209. His justification for recommending that the amendments be incorporated into the body of the Constitution rather than issued as a separate bill of rights was offered in an August 13 speech to the House. The Federalist view that no amendments were necessary was expressed in a letter to Madison from an unidentified writer who signed the letter "Pacificus."

41. Rutland, vol. 12, p. 201.

42. Ibid.

43. Schwartz, vol. 5, p. 1027.

44. Barron v. Baltimore, 7 Peters 243.

CHAPTER 3: THE MILITIA—THEN AND NOW

1. Matloff, p. 101.

2. Quoted in Robert W. Coakley, *The Role of Federal Military Forces in Domestic Disorders, 1789–1876*, p. 7.

3. Tansill, p. 1055.

4. Hyneman and Lutz, vol. 2, pp. 837, 1124.

5. Matloff, p. 19.

6. Ibid., chap. 5, p. 141.

7. Ibid., p. 149.

8. Ibid., p. 166.

9. Ibid., p. 181.

10. Ibid., pp. 184–85.

11. Ibid., chap. 9.

12. Ibid., pp. 192, 282.

13. Ibid., pp. 108, 287, 350–51.

14. Ibid., pp. 290, 367.

15. Ibid., pp. 367, 375.

16. Ibid., p. 411.

17. Executive Office of the President, *Budget of the United States Government, Fiscal Year 1990*, sec. 5, pp. 10–12.

18. Commager and Cantor, vol. 1, p. 174.

19. Philip S. Foner, ed., *The Complete Writings of Thomas Paine*, vol. 1, pp. 20–21.

20. Quoted in Nathaniel Peffer, *America's Place in the World*, p. 11.

21. Commager and Cantor, vol. 1, p. 174.

22. Ibid., pp. 236–37.

23. What came to be known as the Monroe Doctrine was a statement of policy included in President Monroe's December 2, 1823, annual message to Congress; see Commager and Cantor, vol. 1, pp. 235–37. The use of American military forces abroad is documented in House of Representatives, Committee on International Relations, *Background Information on the Use of U.S. Armed Forces in Foreign Countries*.

24. A. Whitney Griswold, *The Far Eastern Policy of the United States*, p. 6.

25. Charles I. Bevens, comp., *Treaties and Other International Agreements of the United States of America, 1776–1949*, vol. 6, p. 649.

26. Griswold, p. 5.

27. The British treaty is in Fred L. Israel, ed., *Major Peace Treaties of Modern History 1648–1967*, vol. 2, pp. 1065–73. For the American treaty, see Bevens, vol. 6, pp. 647–70.

28. Griswold, p. 5.

29. Library of Congress, Congressional Research Service, *Instances of Use of United States Armed Forces Abroad, 1798–1989*.

30. Griswold, p. 3.

31. T. A. Critchley, *A History of Police in England and Wales*, p. 35.

32. Ibid., pp. 42–43.

33. Jonathan Rubinstein, *City Police*, pp. 11–13.

34. Stanford J. Ungar, *FBI*, p. 39.

35. Ibid., p. 40.

36. Ronald Reagan, *A Time for Choosing*, p. 57.

37. Planned Parenthood v. Casey, No. 91–744, 29 June 1992, slip opinion, p. 12.

CHAPTER 4: GUNS AND THE LAW

1. See chap. 2, note 6.

2. Poore, p. 1541.

3. Ibid., p. 1877.

4. Stephen P. Halbrook, *A Right to Bear Arms: State and Federal Bills of Rights and Constitutional Guarantees*, p. 94.

5. Halbrook, *That Every Man Be Armed*, p. 64.

6. Ibid., p. 72.

7. Alexander Hamilton, John Jay, and James Madison, *The Federalist*, No. 46. Madison obviously conceived the population to total approximately 3 million, whereas by 1787, it was probably in excess of 3.5 million. The first official census, taken in 1790, set the figure flightly over 3.9 million.

8. All quotations from state constitutions written or revised after 1860 or continuing unchanged from earlier times are taken from *Constitutions of the United States, National and State*, 7 vols., revised, edited by Shirley S. Abrahamson, published for the Legislative Drafting Research Foundation of Columbia University.

9. The islands were annexed by the United States in 1898, five years after sugar planter Sanford B. Dole incited a revolt against Queen Liliuokalani and declared himself president of Hawaii. After annexation by the United States, Dole was appointed governor of the Territory of Hawaii until 1903, when he was made U.S. district court judge for the territory.

10. This provision was deleted by an amendment reported in the 1979 collection of state constitutions cited in note 8.

11. Poore, pp. 103, 318.

12. Halbrook, *That Every Man Be Armed,* pp. 57–58.

13. Marquis James, *The Life of Andrew Jackson.*

14. Franklin E. Zimring and Gordon Hawkins, *The Citizen's Guide to Gun Control,* p. 122.

15. Georgia's amended constitution dates from 1945, Florida's from 1968.

16. Department of the Treasury, Bureau of Alcohol, Tobacco and Firearms, *State Laws and Public Ordinances—Firearms,* pp. v–vii.

17. Except where another source is indicated, all information on state and municipal gun controls is taken from the BATF manual cited in the previous note.

18. Department of the Treasury, Bureau of Alcohol, Tobacco and Firearms, *Federal Laws Relating to Firearms and Ammunition,* p. 2, quoted from Title 18, *U.S. Code,* chap. 44, sec. 922.

19. Zimring and Hawkins.

20. Ibid., p. 133.

21. P.L. 90-618, 82 Stat. 1213. The entire act, together with regulations on commerce in firearms and ammunition, is reproduced in *Federal Laws Relating to Firearms and Ammunition.*

22. Ibid., pp. 5, 9.

23. PPP, 15 June 1989, vol. 1, p. 743. The White House response to my request for a copy of the BATF review ordered by President Bush was to send me Press Secretary Marlin Fitzwater's April 5, 1989, press briefing, which only repeated the announcement of "a temporary suspension of imports of certain semi-automatic weapons."

24. Ibid.

25. WCPD, 3 October 1993, p. 1968.

26. *Firearms State Laws and Published Ordinances,* p. 54.

27. Ibid., p. 3.

28. Ibid., pp. 30, 33.

29. Ibid., p. 33.

30. WP, 17 March 1982; NYT, 19 June 1982.

31. Undated letters circulated in February 1987 and March 1989. Copies are in the author's files.

CHAPTER 5: WHAT THE COURTS HAVE SAID

1. United States v. Cruikshank, 92 U.S. 542 (1876).

2. *Congressional Globe,* 39th Cong., 2d sess., pp. 1088, 2766.

3. United States v. Cruikshank, 92 U.S. 542, cited earlier.

4. Article XI of the Military Code of Illinois, quoted by the Court in Presser v. Illinois, 116 U.S. 252 (1886).

5. Ibid.

6. Ibid.

7. Miller v. Texas, 153 U.S. 812 (1894).

8. Chicago, Burlington and Quincy Railway Co. v. Chicago, 166 U.S. 226 (1897).

9. Gitlow v. New York, 268 U.S. 652 (1925).

10. United States v. Miller, 307 U.S. 174–178 (1939).

11. NYT, 29 June 1981.

12. United States v. Miller, p. 182.

13. "An Act more effectually to provide for the National Defence by establishing an Uniform Militia throughout the United States." 2d Cong., 1st sess., *U.S. Statutes at Large, 1789–1799*, chap. 33, pp. 271–74.

14. "An Act to provide for calling forth the Militia to execute the laws of the Union, suppress insurrections and repel invasions." May 2, 1792, ibid., chap. 28, pp. 264–65.

15. *U.S. Code*, 1982 ed., Title 10, Sec. 311.

16. Cases v. United States, 131 F. 2d 916, 921 (1942).

17. Stevens v. United States, 440 F. 2d 144, 149 (1971).

18. United States v. Decker, 292 F. 2d 89–90 (1961).

19. For the contested portions of Morton Grove ordinance No. 81–11, see Quilici v. Morton Grove, 695 F. 2d 263–64, note 1.

20. Quilici v. Morton Grove, 532 F. Supp. 1169.

21. Quilici v. Morton Grove, 695 F. 2d 261, 271–72 (1982).

22. Ibid., p. 269, quoting Presser v. Illinois, 116 U.S. 252, 265.

23. Quilici v. Morton Grove, 464 U.S. 863 (1983).

24. Sklar v. Byrne, 727 F. 2d 633 (1984).

25. Gavett v. Alexander, 477 F. Supp. 1035 (1979).

26. 10 U.S.C., Sec. 4307-13, 4308(a)(5).

27. Gavett v. Alexander, p. 1050.

28. 114 CR 12291-93, 19 July 1977.

29. Cited in Gavett v. Alexander, p. 1039.

30. Ibid., p. 1043.

31. Ibid., p. 1044.

32. Ibid., p. 1047.

33. Ibid., pp. 1049, 1051.

34. NYT, 19, 25 April 1994.

35. Jack Lenzi, "Semi-Automatics Constitutionally Protected," *American Hunter*, September 1989, pp. 69–70; Allen R. Didgkins 3d, Letter to the Editor, NYT, 23 December 1989.

CHAPTER 6: WHAT THE PUBLIC THINKS

1. Except where otherwise indicated, all polling data are taken from the published volumes of *The Gallup Poll*, 3 volumes (1935–1971, Random House),

and 18 volumes (1972–1992, Scholarly Resources). The 1938 poll is reported in the Random House series, vol. 1, p. 99.

2. Ibid., Random House series, vol. 3, p. 1625.

3. Ibid., vol. 3, pp. 1859–60.

4. Ibid., vol. 3, p. 2077.

5. Ibid., vol. 3, pp. 2108, 2182.

6. Ibid., vol. 3, p. 2182.

7. Ibid., vol. 3, p. 2246.

8. *Gallup Poll*, Scholarly Resources series, 1981 vol., p. 31.

9. *Gallup Poll*, Random House series, vol. 1, p. 52.

10. Ibid., p. 376.

11. Ibid., vol. 2, p. 880.

12. Ibid., 1980 vol., pp. 24–31.

13. Planned Parenthood v. Casey, No. 91-744, 29 June 1992, slip opinion, p. 12.

14. *Gallup Poll*, 1980 vol., p. 31.

15. Ibid., 1987 vol., p. 13.

16. Ibid., 1989 vol., p. 229.

17. *Field and Stream*, September 1989, p. 15.

18. For similar views see Dick Riley, "The President's Column," *American Rifleman*, August 1990, p. 52.

19. *Field and Stream*, September 1989, pp. 15–16.

20. The pros and cons of the Brady and Staggers plans can be found in CR, May 8, 1991, pp. H2819–2876. Provisions cited from the Brady Handgun Violence Protection Act, P.L. 103–159 of 30 November 1993, are in sections 102 and 103 of the act.

21. *Gallup Poll*, 1991 vol., p. 83.

22. Ibid., p. 135.

23. Ibid., 1993 vol., p. 185.

24. Ibid., pp. 214–15.

25. *New York Times/CBS News* poll reported in NYT 23 January 1994.

CHAPTER 7: THE PRACTICE IN OTHER COUNTRIES

1. WP, 28 June 1968.

2. Zhu Taoying, second secretary, Washington Embassy of the People's Republic of China, to author, 24 October 1990.

3. "Control of Firearms and Swords," selected pages supplied by the Washington Embassy of Japan, from a report containing regulations and crime statistics from 1986 to 1989.

4. Japan, National Police Agency, "Keisatso Hakusho 1990."

5. Ibid., p. 43. A member of the Department of Japanese Studies at Bucknell University suggested that *boryokudan* might be translated as "Japanese Mafia."

6. WP, 28 June 1968.

7. F. Bruce McColm, coordinator, *Freedom in the World: Political and Civil Liberties, 1989–1990*.

8. Michel Mont Corniglion, Vice Consul, Brazilian Embassy, to author, 5 November 1990.

9. Horacio Torro Itura, Director General, Policia de Investigaciones de Chile, to author, 16 April 1991.

10. McColm, pp. 68, 70.

11. Raymond D. Gastil, coordinator, *Freedom in the World: Political and Civil Liberties, 1987–1988*, pp. 290–91.

12. Letter and summary of Polish laws and regulations from Professor Lech Falandysz, Director of the Institute of Justice, Ministry of Justice, 29 March 1991.

13. Tad Szulc, "Dispatches from Eastern Europe," *National Geographic*, March 1991, p. 15.

14. Zákonem č. 147/1983 SB., ve znění zákona č. 49/1990 SB., o abraních a střevlivu. I am grateful to Tereza Mauerova for a translation of this material, printed in the Czech language, which I received from the Ministry of the Interior of the Czech and Slovak Federal Republic under a covering letter dated 1 January 1991. This information is presumed still to apply to the Czech Republic, although it may no longer reflect conditions in now independent Slovakia.

15. Ibid.

16. Personal interview with Tereza Mauerova, 6 July 1992.

17. Letter and summary, "Gun Control in Switzerland," from Daniel Grunenfelder, Consulate General of Switzerland, to author, 7 November 1990.

18. Ibid.

19. Swiss Federal Statistical Office, "Statistical Data on Switzerland," pp. 2, 24.

20. Letter from Robert J. Sieben, Press and Cultural Affairs Secretary, Royal Netherlands Embassy, to author, 7 December 1990.

21. Ibid.

22. National Swedish Council on Crime Prevention, *The Swedish Penal Code* (1984), p. 13.

23. Ibid., p. 12.

24. Ibid., p. 71.

25. Ibid., p. 75.

26. Lars Dolmen, ed., *Crime Trends in Sweden 1988*, pp. 37–40.

27. Ibid., p. 39.

28. Olof H. Wikstrom, *The Development of the Use of Weapons at Violent Crimes, 1970–1987*.

29. Letter and summary of "Regulations Regarding Fire Arms in the Federal Republic of Germany," Elke Czempinski, Vice Consul, Consulate General of the Federal Republic of Germany to author, 29 October 1990.

30. Great Britain COI, Reference Services, "The Control of Firearms in Britain," p. 1.

31. Ibid., p. 2.

32. Ibid., p. 4.

33. Ibid., p. 4.

34. U.S. Dept. of Justice, Bureau of Statistics, *Handgun Crime Victims*; Great Britain HMSO, "Criminal Statistics, England and Wales, 1988," Table 3.1.

35. Baxter, J., and Koffman, L., eds., *Police, the Constitution and the Community*, p. 192.

36. Ibid., p. 194.

37. Ibid., p. 173.

38. Ibid.; see pp. 197–99 for the complete guidelines, which were reproduced by permission from the Home Office.

39. Ibid., p. 199.

40. Canada Department of Justice, *Gun Control in Canada*, p. 2.

41. Ibid., p. 6.

42. Elizabeth Scarff, *Evaluation of the Canadian Gun Control Legislation: Executive Summary*, p. 2.

43. Canada Ministry of the Solicitor General, *Firearms Control in Canada: An Evaluation*, pp. 2, 31, 35.

44. Ibid., p. 3.

45. NYT, 17 October 1991.

46. Canada Department of Justice, "Summary of Major Points in Bill C-17 (Firearms Control)." A copy of the 50-page bill was also provided the writer, courtesy of the Canadian Minister of Justice, A. Kim Campbell.

47. Letter from T. J. Baker, Weapons Registry Office, Australian Federal Police, to author, 22 November 1990.

48. Australian Federal Police, *Firearms Registration Requirements Around Australia*.

49. New Zealand, *Arms Act 1983*, p. 7.

50. Ibid., pp. 8. 10.

51. New Zealand, *Firearms Manual, Section 22: The Arms Regulations 1984*, unpaged.

52. Ibid., appendix 1.

53. New Zealand Police, *Arms Code: Firearms Safety Manual*.

54. C.I.H. Forsyth, *Firearms in New Zealand*, p. 38; NYT, 19 October 1991, data from Interpol.

CHAPTER 8: THE PROPAGANDA CAMPAIGN, PRO AND CON: PHASE 1

1. *Gallup Poll*, Random House series, vol. 3, p. 1939.

2. Ibid., vol. 3, pp. 2027, 2077.

3. Ibid., p. 2130.

4. Harriet Van Horne, "Men Who Like Guns," WP, 14 June 1968.

5. NYT, 13 June 1968.

6. *Wall Street Journal*, 18 June 1968; NYT, 15 June 1968.

7. *Wall Street Journal*, 18 June 1968.

8. PPP, 11 January 1968, p. 30.

9. Ibid., 29 January, 7 February 1968, pp. 107, 151–52, 192–94.

10. CR, 23 May 1968, p. 14798.

11. Ibid., 6 June 1968, pp. 16272, 16276.

12. Ibid., p. 16290.

13. Ibid., pp. 16280, 16288, 16290.

14. Ibid., p. 16300. See Omnibus Crime Control and Safe Streets Act of 1968, P.L. 90-351, 82 Stat. 197.

15. PPP, 19 June 1968, pp. 725–28.

16. Ibid., p. 726.

17. In a special survey of public opinion on prevention of violence taken three days after passage of the Crime Control Act, stricter gun laws headed the list of recommended actions. *Gallup Poll*, Random House Series, vol. 3, p. 2130.

18. CR, 17 July 1968, pp. 21783–84.

19. Ibid., p. 21792.

20. Ibid.

21. Ibid., pp. 21792–93.

22. Ibid., 24 July 1968, pp. 23094–96.

23. Ibid., 18 September 1968, p. 27492.

24. Ibid., 10 October 1968, p. 30583.

25. Ibid., pp. 30582–86.

26. Ibid., p. 30587.

27. PPP, 1968–69, vol. 2, pp. 1059–60.

28. Letter to the editor, NYT, 26 August 1972.

29. NYT, 23 November 1973.

30. H.R. 40, H.R. 3202, H.R. 3532, H.R. 8229, reported in CR, vol. 121, part 1, p. 145; ibid., part 3, pp. 3662, 3921; ibid., part 16, p. 20890.

31. See H.R. 40 in previous note. The radio debate and subsequent comment were reported in NYT, 14 May 1975.

32. NYT, 14 May 1975.

33. CR, 1975, see S. 2186, p. 25076, and S. 141, p. 388.

34. Ibid., part 19, pp. 25076–77; text of bill, pp. 25077–84.

35. Ibid.; part 1, p. 389.

36. PPP, 1972, p. 715.

37. PPP, 1973, pp. 59–60.

38. Ibid., 6 May 1975, vol. 1, p. 651; 22 September 1975, vol. 2, p. 1510.

39. NYT, 3 March 1976.

40. B. Bruce Briggs, "The Great American Gun War," *The Public Interest*, Fall 1976, pp. 37–62.

41. Ibid., p. 62.

42. NYT, 15 April 1977.

43. Donald Bruce Johnson, comp., *National Party Platforms*, vol. 2, pp. 742, 751, 807, 869, 931, 972.

44. NYT, 27 May, 8 June 1978; "BATF Proposes Firearms Regulations; NRA Threatens Reprisal," *Handgun Control News*, May 1978.

45. NYT, 8 April 1979; National Coalition to Ban Handguns, circular letter, May 1979; *Handgun Control News*, April/May 1979.

CHAPTER 9: PROPAGANDA: PHASE 2

1. H.R. 40, 94th Cong., 1st sess., Testimony of Jonathan B. Bingham before the Subcommittee on Crime of the House Judiciary Committee, 20 February 1975; NYT, 21 February 1975.

2. WCPD, 7 February 1984, p. 184.

3. PPP, 22 April, 16 June 1981, pp. 373, 521–22.

4. 1980 Republican Platform, p. 24.

5. 1980 Democratic Platform, p. 18.

6. *Congressional Insight,* 26 September 1980.

7. Allen Ertel to author, 20 October 1980. Ertel's reference to Pennsylvania's gun-control law as "one of the strongest in the country" was based on the fact that a permit is required of anyone who wishes to purchase a gun. However, once that permit is obtained, the holder may purchase, and resell, as many guns as he wishes.

8. NYT, 4 August 1980.

9. NYT, 2 April 1981; PPP, 16 June 1981, pp. 521–22; R. Emmett Tyrrell, Jr., "Liberals Aren't Serious about Gun Control," WP, 6 April 1981.

10. NYT, 5 April 1981.

11. Ibid.

12. NYT, 4 May 1981.

13. Ibid.

14. WP, 23 July 1981.

15. U.S. Senate, Committee on Appropriations, *Proposed Dissolution of Bureau of Alcohol, Tobacco and Firearms,* 97th Cong., 2d sess., p. 1.

16. Ibid., pp. 245–46.

17. NYT, 18 September 1981.

18. Ibid.

19. WP, 12 August 1981. Announcement of the appointment of a task force was made by Vice President George Bush, PPP, 6 April 1981, p. 328.

20. PPP, 17 October 1981, p. 956.

21. PPP, 22 April, 16 June 1981, pp. 373, 521–22.

22. The letter was reproduced in WP, 24 May 1982.

23. This amendment was inserted into P.L. 97–377, whose principal purpose was to provide for continuing appropriations for fiscal year 1983. See President Reagan's statement in PPP, 27 January 1983, p. 126.

24. U.S. Senate. Committee on the Judiciary, *Federal Firearms Owners Protection Act,* Report No. 97-476, 18 June 1982, p. 1.

25. Ibid., pp. 1–2.

26. Ibid., pp. 17–22, 55–59.

27. WP, 21 April; *Congressional Insight,* 7 September; NYT, 16 March 1984.

28. NYT, 27 October 1984.

29. NCBH, *News and Views,* Spring/Summer 1983, identified the bullet as Teflon coated KTW but did not name the manufacturer. President Reagan's address included praise for NRA's successful fight against California's Proposition 15 to make control of handguns a state law, support for anticontrol Senators Hatch, McClure and Volkmer, and a reminder that the Second Amendment prohibits Congress from interfering with the citizen's right to bear arms. See PPP, 6 May 1983, pp. 659–65.

30. *Congressional Insight,* 12 August 1983.

31. P.L. 98-473, 98 Stat. 2139.

32. P.L. 99-408, 28 August 1986.

33. WCPD, 28 August 1986, pp. 1130–31. For a summary of the action in the Senate and House, see NYT, 7 March 1986.

34. P.L. 99-308, 19 May 1986.

35. Interview with *New York Times* reporters, WCPD, 23 March 1986, p. 406.

36. P.L. 99-308, sec. 103(g)(1)(A).

37. P.L. 99-308, sec. 926A.

38. WP, 22 August 1987.

39. See AP report published 15 June 1991 in the Sunbury (Pa.) *Daily Item*. An inquiry to the Washington embassy of the Holy See brought a reply that as of 21 May 1992 that office was "not aware of any response by the Congregation [for the causes of saints] in this matter."

40. WCPD, 5 November 1988, p. 1454. For similar comments in earlier years or in other campaign speeches made on behalf of Republican candidates for the Senate or House, see WCPD or PPP indexes under Law Enforcement and Crime: Gun Control.

41. PPP, 16 February 1989, vol. 1, p. 105; Donnie Radcliffe, *Simply Barbara Bush*, pp. 59, 62–63.

42. PPP, 15 September 1989, vol. 2, p. 1199.

43. Donnie Radcliffe, *Simply Barbara Bush*, p. 59.

44. Treasury Department, BATF, *State Laws*, p. 18.

45. Ibid.

46. United States v. Cruikshank, 92 U.S. 542, cited earlier; NYT, 23 May 1992.

47. *American Hunter*, July 1989, p. 55; CR (daily), 8 February 1989, p. S 51322, 28 February, p. H 468, 1 March, p. H 492, 11 April, p. S 3614.

48. House of Representatives, Committee on the Judiciary, Subcommittee on Crime, *Hearings: Semiautomatic Assault Weapons Act of 1989*, pp. 1–2.

49. Ibid., pp. 352–53.

50. Ibid., pp. 355, 357, 367–69.

51. Ibid., p. 351.

52. *American Rifleman*, April 1990, p. 51. See also, Jack Anderson and Dale Van Atta, "Rifle Association Up to Old Tricks," *Sunbury Daily Item*, 13 April 1990.

53. *The Antidrug, Assault Weapons Limitation Act of 1989*, 3 October 1989, p. 5.

54. *American Hunter*, July 1989, p. 54; CR, 15 November 1989, pp. E 3830–31, 13 September 1990, p. E 2826.

55. *American Hunter*, September 1989, p. 7.

56. Ibid., p. 68.

57. MacNeil/Lehrer News Hour, 11 April 1990, transcript, pp. 5–9.

58. NYT, 21 May 1990.

59. NYT, 28 May 1990.

60. *American Rifleman*, May 1990, p. 42.

61. Wayne LaPierre, "Parade Poll: New Twist, Old Results," and Paul H. Blackman, "High Court Comments on 'Rights of the People,'" *American Rifleman*, June 1990, pp. 48ff.; Warren E. Berger, "The Right to Bear Arms," *Parade*, 14 January 1990, p. 4.

62. CR (daily), 14 June 1990, pp. S 7963–65.

63. Undated circular letter distributed August 1990.

64. *American Rifleman*, October 1990.

65. Ibid., December 1990, pp. 46–47. The "institute" is the NRA Institute for Legislative Action, the organization's lobbying arm.

66. Ronald Reagan, "Why I'm for the Brady Bill," NYT, 29 March 1991, copyright © 1991 by The New York Times Company. Reprinted by permission.

67. WCPD, 8 May 1991, p. 580.

68. Message to Congress, WCPD, 11 March 1991, pp. 289–90.

69. WCPD, 15 May, 30 May, 2 October 1991, pp. 612, 691, 1384.

70. Ibid., 1 November 1991, p. 1576.

71. *CQ Weekly Report*, 21 March 1992. See Conference Committee Report 102-405 on H.R. 3371 and the "Bush Bill," S. 2305.

72. WCPD, 26 November 1991, p. 1732.

73. NYT, 20 March 1992.

74. James Brady letter to Handgun Control members, undated, circulated March 1992. Neal Knox had been a member of the Board of Directors of NRA but had been ousted in a bitter internal fight. In the January 1991 issue of *American Rifleman*, Executive Vice President J. Warren Cassidy printed an open letter to NRA members in which he warned that Knox was "operating a lobbying firm that competes with the NRA" for funds and for influence in Congress, and had been attacking NRA officials ever since he had been fired in 1982 "for mismanagement of NRA's legislative program."

75. Republican Platform, 1992, p. 23, published in pamphlet form by the Republican National Committee, Washington, D.C.

76. 1992 Democratic Platform, p. 11, published in pamphlet form by the Democratic National Committee.

77. NYT, 1 February 1992.

78. *Las Vegas Review Journal*, 8 February 1992.

79. NYT, 9–20 March 1992.

80. "Consumers' Guide to Gun Culture," NYT, 30 March 1992.

81. NYT, 7 May 1992.

82. Ibid., 7 May, 30 June 1992.

83. The 1992 presidential debates were reported, verbatim, in most of the country's major newspapers.

84. NYT, 1 November 1992.

85. WCPD, vol. 29 (1993), pp. 174, 220, 259–62, 339, 1568, 1603–5, 1628. For text of directives from President Clinton to the treasury secretary, see WCPD, 11 August 1993, pp. 1605–7.

86. NYT, 27 November 1993.

87. Ibid., 28, 30 December 1993, 6 January 1994.

88. Ibid., 2 January 1994.

89. *Miami Herald*, 1 January 1994; NYT, 23 December 1993, 2, 6 January 1994; MacNeil/Lehrer News Hour, 5 January 1994.

90. "Proposed Comprehensive Bill of Handgun Control, Inc.," n.d.

91. Charley Reese, "Brady Bill II: A Conspiracy to Deprive Honest Americans of Liberty," *Orlando Sentinel*, 10 March 1994.

92. Richard M. Aborn to author, 21 March 1994.

93. Charley Reese to author, 5 April 1994.

94. Vice President Gore's undated letter was received by the author 26 April 1994, the same day President Clinton's proposed assault-weapons ban was reported in the *New York Times*.

95. NYT, 6 May 1994.

96. Ibid., 26 August 1994.

CHAPTER 10: WHAT ARE THE ALTERNATIVES?

1. "200 Million Guns," 7-part series, NYT, 8 March–4 April 1992; "Firepower," *Wall Street Journal*, 28 February 1992; "Los Angeles Riots Spurring Big Rise in Sales of Guns," NYT, 14 May, 9 February 1992; Berger, p. 4; Robert C. Byrd, "Crime Control, Not Gun Control," *Congressional Record*, 14 June 1990, S7963–64; Wayne LaPierre, "The 101st Congress Has Ended and Victory Is Ours!", *American Rifleman*, December 1990, p. 46; *The Gallup Poll*, as cited in annual volumes published since 1935; "The News at Six: TV's Grim 1994 Vision," NYT, 14 June 1992; *Miami Herald*, 1 January 1994.

2. CR (daily), 8 May 1991, H2822, 2855–56.

3. "Violent Crime Control and Law Enforcement Act of 1991," *Conference Report 102-405* (on H.R. 3371), p. 23.

4. Cited by Representative Mel Levine of California in CR (daily), 8 May 1991, H2876.

5. *Field and Stream*, September 1989, pp. 16–17.

6. Joe Foss, "The President's Column," *American Rifleman*, July 1990, p. 52.

7. *Handgun Control News*, March/April 1979, p. 1. In Gavett v. Alexander (477 F. Supp. 1035, 1049, 1051), a federal court upheld the NCBH challenge, declaring invalid that section of the law "which requires membership in the National Rifle Association as a precondition to the purchase of Army surplus rifles" on the grounds that it "unconstitutionally deprives plaintiffs of the equal protection of the laws in violation of the Fourteenth Amendment to the Constitution."

8. *Gallup Poll*, 1990, pp. 122–26; 1991, pp. 82–84, 116–18, 135.

9. U.S. Department of Justice, *Attorney General's Program for Improving the Nation's Crinminal History Records and Identifying Felons Who Attempt to Purchase Firearms* (March 1991), p. 1.

10. U.S. Department of Justice, *Identifying Persons, Other than Felons, Ineligible to Purchase Firearms: A Feasibility Study* (May 1990), p. iii.

11. *Gallup Poll*, 1991 vol., p. 118.

12. Senate Report 101-160 on S. 747, 3 October 1989, p. 16.

13. CR (daily), 8 May 1991, p. H 2819.

14. Ibid., p. H 2856.

15. Ibid., 8 May 1991, p. H 2823.

16. See President Bush's proposed "good faith" exception to the rule that evidence obtained in violation of the Fourth Amendment may not be used in court, and the House Conference Report on that subject in the Violent Crime Control and Law Enforcement Act of 1991. PPP, 15 May 1991, vol. 1, pp. 563–64; House Conference Report 102-405, 27 November 1991, p. 22.

17. U.S. Department of Justice, Federal Bureau of Investigation, *Uniform Crime Reports for the United States, 1990*, p. iii.

18. Ibid.

19. Treasury Department, BATF, *State Laws and Published Ordinances—Firearms*, 20th ed., 1994, p. 18.

20. WP, 9 November 1982.

21. *Wall Street Journal*, 28 February 1992.

22. These events were reported by every branch of the media in gruesome detail all through the months of April and May 1992.

23. Franklin E. Zimring, "Guns, Guns Everywhere—Strategies for Arms Control," NYT, 4 January 1991.

24. Florida Statutes, 90.173-74 (1991).

25. *Orlando Sentinel*, 17, 21 February, 29 March 1991.

26. NYT, 31 December 1992.

27. *Orlando Sentinel*, 27 December 1991.

28. Ibid., 20 August 1991.

29. Associated Press report, Sunbury, Pa., *Daily Item*, 19 August 1992.

30. Department of the Treasury, BATF, *State Laws*, p. 5.

31. *Journal of the American Medical Association*, 10 June 1992.

32. Scarff, p. 1.

33. Canadian Parliament, Bill C-117, approved 5 December 1991.

34. Ronald Reagan, *Ronald Reagan Talks to America*, p. 173.

35. Some would prefer to say Jews and non-Jews, but the fact is that most white supremacist groups parade as Christians.

36. NYT, 3, 29 March 1994.

37. NYT, 19 December 1993, 26 August 1994.

38. NYT, 10 June 1993.

39. Handgun Control, "Progress Report," 2-page flier, December 1992; "Comment: Under the Gun," *New Yorker*, 22 March 1993; NYT, 26 April 1993; Sunbury, Pa., *Daily Item*, 2 April, 21 June 1993.

40. WCPD, 17 February 1993, p. 220.

41. *New Yorker*, see note 39; NYT, 8 July 1993.

42. "The Media and Images of War: Perception Versus Reality," *Defense Monitor*, vol. 23, no. 4, 1994, p. 1. This entire issue is devoted to an analysis of the public impact of these factors:

- The popular interpretation of America's history "celebrates" the westward movement of the frontier through war and conquest.
- Films and television programs about war and the frontier perpetuate the myth that war and violence are the American way to achieve success.
- Post–World War II Americans, who grew up with film and television, developed the expectation that the cavalry, western lawmen, and combat heroes always "win." Violence by "good" Americans was always portrayed as producing positive results.
- This biased view of America's past falsely mythologizes the "man with the gun" as a representative, admirable American.
- In modern war the military both creates and manages the film images the public sees. Such control can make war seem precise and largely bloodless.

43. Justification in Senate bill S.1882 (1994).

44. H. G. Wells, *The Outline of History*, chap. 15.

Bibliography

U.S. GOVERNMENT DOCUMENTS AND PUBLICATIONS

Unless otherwise indicated, all federal documents are published in Washington, D.C., by the Government Printing Office.

Bevens, Charles I., comp. *Treaties and Other International Agreements of the United States of America, 1776–1949*. Vol. 6.

Byrd, Robert C. "Crime Control, Not Gun Control." *Congressional Record*. 14 June 1990. Pp. S 7963–64.

Coakley, Robert W. *The Role of Federal Military Forces in Domestic Disorders, 1789–1876*. Washington: Center of Military History, U.S. Army, 1988.

Congressional Globe. 39th Cong., 2d sess.

Congressional Record. As cited.

Executive Office of the President. *Budget of the United States Government*. Fiscal Year 1990.

Federal Register, Office of. *Public Papers of the Presidents of the United States*. As cited.

———. *Weekly Compilation of Presidential Documents*. As cited.

House of Representatives. Committee on the Judiciary. Subcommittee on Crime. *Hearings: Semiautomatic Assault Weapons Act of 1989*.

———. Committee on International Relations. *Background Information on the Use of U.S. Armed Forces in Foreign Countries*. 1975.

House-Senate. *Violent Crime Control and Law Enforcement Act of 1991*. Conference Report 102-405 (on H.R. 3371).

Justice, Department of. *Attorney General's Program for Improving the Nation's Criminal History Records and Identifying Felons Who Attempt to Purchase Firearms*. March 1991.

———. *Identifying Persons, Other than Felons, Ineligible to Purchase Firearms: A Feasibility Study*. May 1990.

Justice, Department of. Bureau of Investigation. *Uniform Crime Reports for the United States, 1990*.

———. Bureau of Statistics. *Handgun Crime Victims*. June 1990.

Library of Congress. *Letters of Delegates to Congress 1774–1789*. 17+ vols.

———. Congressional Research Service. *Instances of Use of United States Armed Forces Abroad, 1798–1989*. 4 December 1989.

Matloff, Maurice, ed. *American Military History*. Revised ed. Washington: Office of the Chief of Military History. 1973.

Poore, Ben Perley, comp. *The Federal and State Constitutions, Colonial Charters, and Other Organic Laws of the United States*. Washington: Government Printing Office, 1878.

Senate. Committee on Appropriations. *Proposed Dissolution of Bureau of Alcohol, Tobacco and Firearms*. 97th Cong., 2d sess., 1982.

———. Committee on the Judiciary. *Federal Firearms Owners Protection Act*. Report No. 97-476. 18 June 1982.

———. *The Antidrug, Assault Weapons Limitation Act of 1989*. Report No. 101-160. 3 October 1989.

Smith, Paul H., comp. *English Defenders of American Freedom 1774–1778*. Washington: Library of Congress, 1972.

Statutes at Large. As cited.

Tansill, Charles C., ed. *Documents Illustrative of the Formation of the Union of American States*. Washington: Government Printing Office, 1927.

Treasury, Department of, Bureau of Alcohol, Tobacco and Firearms (BATF). *Federal Laws Relating to Firearms and Ammunition*. AFT P 5300, 1977.

———. *State Laws and Public Ordinances—Firearms*. 20th ed. (1994).

United States Code. As cited.

COURT CASES

Barron v. Baltimore, 7 Peters 243 (1833).
Cases v. United States, 131 F. 2d 916, 921 (1942).
Chicago, Burlington and Quincy Railway Co. v. Chicago, 166 U.S. 226 (1897).
Gavett v. Alexander, 477 F. Supp. 1035 (1979).
Gitlow v. New York, 268 U.S. 652 (1925).
Miller v. Texas, 153 U.S. 812 (1894).
Planned Parenthood v. Casey, No. 91-744, 29 June 1992, slip opinion.
Presser v. Illinois, 116 U.S. 255 (1886).
Quilici v. Morton Grove, 532 F. Supp. 1169.
Quilici v. Morton Grove, 695 F. 2d 216.
Quilici v. Morton Grove, 464 U.S. 863 (1983).
Sklar v. Byrne, 727 F. 2d 633 (1984).

Stevens v. United States, 440 F. 2d 144 (1971).
United States v. Cruikshank, 92 U.S. 542 (1876).
United States v. Decker, 292 F. 2d 89 (1961).
United States v. Miller, 307 U.S. 174 (1939).

PERSONAL CORRESPONDENCE

Australian Federal Police. T. J. Baker, Weapons Registry, to author, 22 November 1990.
Brazilian Embassy. Michael Mont Corniglion, Vice Consul, to author, 5 November 1990.
Canadian Minister of Justice. A. Kim Campbell to author, 19 February 1992.
Chile. Horacio Toro Iturra, Director General, Policia de Investigaciones, to author, 16 April 1991.
Czech and Slovak Federal Republic. JUDr. Josef Svoboda, Ministry of the Interior, to author, 16 January 1991.
Ertel, Allen, to author, 20 October 1980.
German Federal Republic. Elke Czempinski, Vice Counsul, New York Consulate, to author, 29 October 1990.
Netherlands Embassy. Robert J. Sieben, Press and Cultural Affairs, to author, 7 December 1990.
New Zealand Police. National Headquarters. Tom Nunann, Firearms Advisory Officer, to author, 22 November 1990.
People's Republic of China, Washington Embassy. Zhu Taoying, Second Secretary, to author, 24 October 1990.
Polish Institute of Justice. Professor Lech Falandysz, Director, to author, 29 March 1991.
Swiss Consulate. Daniel Grunenfelder, Consulate General, to author, 7 November 1990.

GENERAL

Abrahamson, Shirley S., ed. *Constitutions of the United States, National and State.* 7 vols. Revised. Published for the Legislative Drafting Research Foundation of Columbia University. Dobbs Ferry, N.Y.: Oceana Publications, 1989.
Anderson, Jack, and Van Atta, Dale. "Rifle Association Up to Old Tricks." Sunbury *Daily Item,* 13 April 1990.
Australia. Federal Police. *Firearms Manual, Section 22: The Arms Regulations 1984.* Unpaged.
————. *Firearms Registration Requirements around Australia.* N.d.
"BATF Proposes Firearms Regulations; NRA Threatens Reprisal." *Handgun Control News.* May 1978.
Baxter, J., and Koffman, L., eds. *Police, the Constitution and the Community.* Abington, England: Professional Books, 1985.
Berger, Warren E. "The Right to Bear Arms." *Parade,* 14 January 1990.

Blackman, Paul H. "High Court Comments on 'Rights of the People.' " *American Rifleman*, June 1990.

Brady, James, letter to Handgun Control members, undated. Circulated March 1992.

Briggs, B. Bruce. "The Great American Gun War." *The Public Interest*, Fall 1976, pp. 37–62.

Canada. Department of Justice. *Gun Control in Canada*. N.d.

———. "Summary of Major Points in Bill C-17 (Firearms Control)." December 1991.

Canada. Ministry of the Solicitor General. *Firearms Control in Canada, An Evaluation*. Ottawa: Government Publication Centre, 1983.

Commager, Henry Steele, and Cantor, Milton. *Documents of American History*. 2 vols, 10th ed. Englewood Cliffs, N.J.: Prentice Hall, 1988.

Commager, Henry Steele, and Morris, Richard B., *The Spirit of Seventy-Six*. New York: Harper and Row, 1975.

Critchley, T. A. *A History of Police in England and Wales*. London: Constable, 1978.

Czech and Slovak Federal Republic. "Zákonem č. 147/1983 SB., ve znění zákona č. 49/1990 SB., o abraních a střevlivu.

Democratic National Committee. Democratic Platform. 1980, 1992. Washington, D.C.

Dolmen, Lars, ed. *Crime Trends in Sweden 1988*. Stockholm: National Council for Crime Prevention, 1990.

Dumbault, Edward Dumbauld. *The Bill of Rights*. Norman: University of Oklahoma Press, 1957.

Edel, Wilbur. *The Reagan Presidency*. New York: Hippocrene Books, 1992.

Elliot, Jonathan, ed. *The Debates in the Several Conventions on the Adoption of the Federal Constitution as Recommended by the General Convention at Philadelphia in 1787*. 2d ed. 3 vols. Washington: Printed by and for the Editor, 1836.

Foner, Philip S., ed. *The Complete Writings of Thomas Paine*. 2 vols. New York: Citadel Press, 1969.

Forsyth, C.I.H. *Firearms in New Zealand*. Wellington: New Zealand Mountain Safety Council, n.d.

Foss, Joe. "The President's Column." *American Rifleman*, July 1990.

Gallup Poll. 3 vols. (1935–1971). New York: Random House, 1972. 18 vols (1972–1992). Wilmington, Del.: Scholarly Resources, 1979–1993.

Gastil, Raymond D., coordinator. *Freedom in the World: Political and Civil Liberties, 1987–1988*. New York: Freedom House, 1988.

Great Britain. Central Office of Information. Reference Services. "The Control of Firearms in Britain." February 1989.

———. Her Majesty's Stationery Office. "Criminal Statistics, England and Wales, 1988."

Griswold, A. Whitney. *The Far Eastern Policy of the United States*. New York: Harcourt, Brace, 1938.

Halbrook, Stephen P. *A Right to Bear Arms: State and Federal Bills of Rights and Constitutional Guarantees*. Westport, Conn.: Greenwood Press, 1989.

———. *That Every Man Be Armed: The Evolution of a Constitutional Right.* Albuquerque: University of New Mexico Press, 1984.

Hamilton, Alexander; Jay, John; and Madison, James. *The Federalist.* New York: Modern Library, 1937.

Handgun Control. "Proposed Comprehensive Bill of Handgun Control, Inc." Pamphlet. Washington, D.C. 8 December 1993.

Hyneman, Charles S., and Lutz, Donald S. *American Political Writing during the Founding Era 1760–1805.* 2 vols. Indianapolis, Ind.: Liberty Press, 1983.

Israel, Fred L., ed. *Major Peace Treaties of Modern History 1648–1967.* 2 vols. New York: Chelsea House, 1967.

James, Marquis. *The Life of Andrew Jackson.* New York: Bobbs-Merrill, 1938.

Japan, National Police Agency. "Keisatso Hakusho 1990" (White Paper on Police, 1990).

Johnson, Donald Bruce, comp. *National Party Platforms.* 2 vols. Urbana, Ill.: University of Chicago Press, 1978.

Kaminski, John P., and Saladino, Gaspare J., eds. *The Documentary History of the Ratification of the Constitution.* Vols. 8, 13. Madison, Wis.: State Historical Society of Wisconsin, 1976.

LaPierre, Wayne. "The 101st Congress Has Ended and Victory Is Ours!" *American Rifleman,* December 1990.

———. "Parade Poll: New Twist, Old Results." *American Rifleman,* December 1990.

Laurie, Peter. *Scotland Yard: A Study of the Metropolitan Police.* New York: Holt, Rinehart and Winston, 1970.

Lenzi, Jack. "Semi-Automatics Constitutionally Protected." *American Hunter,* September 1989.

Machiavelli, Niccolò. *The Prince.* London: George Routledge, 1883.

MacNeil/Lehrer News Hour, 11 April 1990. Transcript.

Main, Jackson Turner. *The Anti-Federalists: Critics of the Constitution, 1781–1788.* New York: W. W. Norton, 1974.

McColm, F. Bruce, coordinator. *Freedom in the World: Political and Civil Liberties, 1989–1990.* New York: Freedom House, 1990.

National Coalition to Ban Handguns. Circular letter, May 1979.

———. *News and Views.* Spring/Summer 1983.

National Council for Crime Prevention. *The Swedish Penal Code.* Stockholm: Liber Förlag, 1984.

New Zealand. New Zealand Police. *Arms Code: Firearms Safety Manual.* Wellington: TEE JAY Printing, 1989.

Peffer, Nathaniel. *America's Place in the World.* New York: Viking Press, 1947.

Peterson, Merrill D., ed. *Thomas Jefferson: Writings.* New York: Library of America, 1984.

Radcliffe, Donnie. *Simply Barbara Bush.* New York: Warner Books, 1990.

Reagan, Ronald. *Ronald Reagan Talks to America.* Old Greenwich, Conn.: Devin Adair, 1983.

———. *A Time for Choosing.* Chicago: Regnery Gateway, 1983.

———. "Why I'm for the Brady Bill." NYT, 29 March 1991.

Republican National Committee. Republican Platform, 1980, 1992. Washington, D.C.

Rubinstein, Jonathan. City Police. New York: Farrar, Strauss and Giroux, 1973.

Rutland, Robert A., ed., The Papers of James Madison. Vols. 8–12. Charlottesville: University Press of Virginia, 1977.

Scarff, Elizabeth. Evaluation of the Canadian Gun Control Legislation: Executive Summary. Ottawa: Canadian Government Publishing Center, 1983.

Schwartz, Bernard, ed. The Roots of the Bill of Rights. 5 vols. New York: Chelsea House, 1980.

Shalope, Robert E. "The Ideological Origins of the Second Amendment." Journal of American History (December 1982).

Swiss Federal Statistical Office. Statistical Data on Switzerland. Berne, 1989.

Thomson, Basil. The Story of Scotland Yard. New York: Literary Guild, 1936.

"200 Million Guns." 7-part series. NYT, 8 March–4 April 1992.

Tyrell, R. Emmett, Jr. "Liberals Aren't Serious about Gun Control." WP, 6 April 1981.

Ungar, Sanford J. FBI. Boston: Little, Brown, 1976.

Van Horne, Harriet. "Men Who Like Guns." WP, 14 June 1968.

Wikström, Olof H. The Development of the Use of Weapons at Violent Crimes, 1970–1987. Stockholm, 1990.

Zimring, Franklin E. "Guns, Guns Everywhere—Strategies for Arms Control." NYT, 4 January 1991.

Zimring, Franklin E., and Hawkins, Gordon. The Citizen's Guide to Gun Control. New York: Macmillan, 1987.

Index

About the Author

WILBUR EDEL is Professor Emeritus of Political Science at Lehman College of the City University of New York. He is the author of several books, including *Defenders of the Faith* (Praeger, 1987) and *A Constitutional Convention* (Praeger, 1981).

ISBN 0-275-95145-6

9 780275 951450

90000>

EAN

HARDCOVER BAR CODE